100 WINNING DUPL

For the Improving Tournament

new edition

Many competent players are frus._ _.ɔd by an apparent inability to score well at duplicate pairs. No matter how hard they try, the secret of success seems to lie forever beyond reach. The truth is that playing good bridge is not enough to win at pairs. The regular winners are those who have learned to adapt their strategy to take account of the vagaries of match-point scoring. A small shift in emphasis can make a big difference to your results.

In this book Australian expert Ron Klinger shows you how to do it. There are five sections covering constructive bidding, competitive bidding, opening leads, declarer play and defence, and they are full of well-chosen example hands and sound advice. Put these tips into practice and your results are sure to improve.

In this new edition *50 Winning Duplicate Tips* has been expanded to 100 tips. The original tips have been revised and updated, with many examples chosen from recent major national and international tournaments. They have been bolstered by many new tips to reflect modern developments, especially in the area of competitive bidding, and so the book makes an ideal companion to the new edition of *100 Winning Bridge Tips.*

Ron Klinger is a leading international bridge teacher and has represented Australia in many world championships from 1976 to 2003. He has written over forty books, some of which have been translated into Bulgarian, Chinese, Danish, French, Hebrew and Icelandic.

by RON KLINGER *in the Master Bridge Series*

BETTER BRIDGE WITH A BETTER MEMORY • BRIDGE IS FUN
THE POWER OF SHAPE • WHEN TO BID, WHEN TO PASS
*GUIDE TO BETTER CARD PLAY • PLAYING TO WIN AT BRIDGE
*Winner of the 1991 *Book of the Year Award* of the American Bridge Teachers' Association
GUIDE TO BETTER ACOL BRIDGE • 5-CARD MAJORS • POWER ACOL
GUIDE TO BETTER DUPLICATE BRIDGE • CUE-BIDDING TO SLAMS
BRIDGE CONVENTIONS, DEFENCES & COUNTERMEASURES
100 WINNING BRIDGE TIPS • 50 MORE WINNING BRIDGE TIPS
100 WINNING DUPLICATE TIPS • ACOL BRIDGE MADE EASY
THE MODERN LOSING TRICK COUNT • ACOL BRIDGE FLIPPER
IMPROVE YOUR BRIDGE MEMORY • PRACTICAL SLAM BIDDING
RON KLINGER'S MASTER CLASS • DUPLICATE BRIDGE FLIPPER
LAW OF TOTAL TRICKS FLIPPER • 5-CARD MAJORS FLIPPER
20 GREAT CONVENTIONS FLIPPER • BASIC ACOL BRIDGE FLIPPER
THE MODERN LOSING TRICK COUNT FLIPPER
BID BETTER, MUCH BETTER AFTER OPENING 1NT
RON KLINGER ANSWERS YOUR BRIDGE QUERIES

with Pat Husband and Andrew Kambites
BASIC BRIDGE: The Guide to Good Acol Bidding and Play

with David Bird
KOSHER BRIDGE • KOSHER BRIDGE 2
THE RABBI'S MAGIC TRICK: More Kosher Bridge

with Andrew Kambites
BRIDGE CONVENTIONS FOR YOU
CARD PLAY MADE EASY 1: Safety Plays and Endplays
CARD PLAY MADE EASY 2: Know Your Suit Combinations
CARD PLAY MADE EASY 3: Trump Management
CARD PLAY MADE EASY 4: Timing and Communication
HOW GOOD IS YOUR BRIDGE HAND?
UNDERSTANDING THE CONTESTED AUCTION
UNDERSTANDING THE UNCONTESTED AUCTION
UNDERSTANDING DUPLICATE PAIRS
UNDERSTANDING SLAM BIDDING

with Hugh Kelsey
NEW INSTANT GUIDE TO BRIDGE

with Mike Lawrence
OPENING LEADS FOR ACOL PLAYERS
OPENING LEADS FLIPPER

with Derek Rimington
IMPROVE YOUR BIDDING AND PLAY

100 WINNING DUPLICATE TIPS

new edition

Ron Klinger

CASSELL
IN ASSOCIATION WITH
PETER CRAWLEY

First published in Great Britain 1991
in association with Peter Crawley
by Victor Gollancz Ltd
Fifth impression 1999

This new edition first published 2003
Second impression 2004
in association with Peter Crawley
by Cassell
Wellington House, 125 Strand, London WC2R 0BB
an imprint of the Orion Publishing Group

A catalogue record for this book
is available from the British Library

ISBN 0-304-36612-9

Typeset by Modern Bridge Publications
P.O. Box 140, Northbridge NSW 1560, Australia

Printed and bound in Great Britain by Clays Ltd, St Ives plc

www.orionbooks.co.uk

Contents

Introduction

100 Winning Bridge Tips (seventh impression 2000, new edition 2003) was written for the improving player to try to boost the general level of bridge, whether it was for rubber bridge, teams play or match-pointed pairs. This book is aimed at pairs players since most tournament players find themselves playing match-pointed pairs either exclusively or most of the time. Teams play is popular at the higher levels, but at the average club there would be at least twenty pairs sessions for every session of teams.

100 Winning Duplicate Tips is designed for the improving tournament player. Pairs play is quite different from rubber bridge and the secret of winning at pairs is bound up with the scoring method. At rubber you are rewarded by the score you obtain. The size of the score is relevant. At pairs, the size of the score is not relevant in any absolute sense. The only question is, 'How many pairs did your score beat?' Not by how much did you beat them, but simply is your score better than theirs? You are given points for each pair that you beat on each board. The points you receive are the same whether you beat them narrowly or whether you outscore them by a lot.

The yardstick for success is thus not the size of the score but the frequency of outscoring your opponents. Your real opponents at pairs are not the players against whom you play each deal, but the other pairs who are sitting in the same direction as you and against whose results your scores will be compared.

Winning strategy, whether it is in the bidding or the play, centres on how often a particular action will succeed in the long run. Methods which apply only rarely, no matter how effectively, have given way to systems and conventions which deal with the regular, commonplace situations that arise day-in, day-out in duplicate tournaments. As long as your methods and your style tend to produce winning results more than 50% of the time, they should be retained. Areas of your system and conventions which succeed less frequently need to be discarded.

In this new edition several of the original tips have been amalgamated and many new tips have been added. A word about terminology: HCP = high card points, LHO = left-hand opponent, RHO = right-hand opponent, + = 'or more' or 'or longer', according to context, RKCB = Roman Key Card Blackwood.

The *Tips* are aimed at providing the best strategy for your bidding, play and defence at match-pointed pairs. The expert pairs will be familiar with the ideas in these tips. Equally, the expert is not eager to share that knowledge with you, but prefers to maintain an edge as long as possible.

I cannot give you a better recommendation than that the methods and style in this book are the ones my partners and I use. If you can apply even 50% of the advice in these *Tips*, you will narrow the gap between yourself and the expert. You will find your scores improving and you will be winning more sessions and more tournaments. There is nothing that matches the euphoria of winning. And, who knows? Perhaps it will not be long before you find yourself finishing in front of your club's accepted top players. Perhaps they will be coming to you to ask how you found the winning move. If so, do not lend them a copy of this book. Make them go out and buy their own.

Ron Klinger, 1991, 2003

Part 1: CONSTRUCTIVE BIDDING

Success at duplicate requires an understanding of the nature of the scoring. You are not rewarded for the score you achieve. You gain only if your score is better than the scores of other pairs, no matter by how little. Bidding and making a slam might be worth nothing. If you make 6♡ vulnerable for +1430 you could score zero match-points if the other pairs in your direction make thirteen tricks for +1460 or 6NT for +1440 or if they bid and make a grand slam. Likewise, one down in 3NT might be a top score if the other pairs are going two down, three down or more. It is not the score that matters but how that score compares with the other pairs holding the same cards as you and partner.

This leads to the strategy of duplicate bidding. Safety is not your primary concern but the frequency of gain. How often will your action produce a positive result rather than a negative one? The size of the gain is rarely critical. Gaining 50 points four times but losing 800 once would be anathema to rubber bridge players and to teams' players, but at match-pointed pairs that would be an excellent approach. If the success rate exceeds 50%, it is a sound strategy even though the size of the loss might be horrendous when it occurs.

Basic strategy at pairs is to avoid 5♣ and 5♢ at all costs if 3NT is feasible. If the choice is between a minor suit game or 3NT, ask yourself not whether 3NT will make or whether it is safe but whether it could make? If the answer is 'Yes, it could make,' then that is the contract for you. On the other hand, almost always choose 4♡ or 4♠ ahead of 3NT as long as your side has eight or more trumps. If your major suit fit is only seven cards, then choose 3NT unless the bidding has revealed that 3NT is unsound.

The following tips for opening and responding supplement this basic strategy.

1 What action would you take as dealer, neither side vulnerable, with the following hands?

(A)	(B)	(C)
♠ K Q 6 4	♠ A 8 6 5 2	♠ A 9 7 6 3
♡ 5	♡ 5	♡ 5
◇ A J 8 6 3 2	◇ 7 3	◇ 8
♣ 7 5	♣ A Q 6 4 2	♣ A J 9 6 4 2

The basic yardstick for opening the bidding is 12 HCP. Unless there are at least two serious defects in the hand, open the bidding if you have 12 HCP or more. You should also open the bidding with fewer HCP if you have good shape as compensation. A good test, devised by Marty Bergen of the USA, is the Rule of 20: Add your HCP to the number of cards in your two longest suits. If the total comes to 20 or more, open the bidding. With some qualifications, this is a sound approach at pairs or at teams bridge.

Applying the Rule of 20 you should open each of the above hands. Bid 1◇, your longest suit, with (A). If partner responds 1♡, you will rebid 1♠, but over 1NT or 2♣, your rebid is 2◇.

With (B) start with 1♠, the higher-ranking when you hold two five-card suits. Over 1NT, rebid 2♣, but over 2◇ or 2♡ you are not strong enough for 3♣ and so you should rebid 2♠.

Some prefer to open 1♣ with five spades and five clubs. That will work if the opponents promise not to intervene, but meek opponents are hard to find these days. If you open 1♣ and they bid and raise a red suit to the three-level or higher, will you introduce your spades then with such a weak opening? It is better to open 1♠ and risk missing clubs than to open 1♣ and risk missing spades.

Open your longest suit, 1♣, with (C). Over 1◇ or 1♡, rebid 1♠ and bid the spades again on the next round if partner has not shown support for spades yet. Given that you open 1♠ with 5-5 in the black suits, the sequence of 1♣, then spades and spades again indicates five spades and hence six or more clubs.

Tip 1: Use the Rule of 20 as a base for deciding whether to open.

2 What action would you take as dealer, neither side vulnerable, with the following hands?

(A)	(B)	(C)
♠ A 8 6	♠ K 8 6	♠ Q J 6 5 2
♡ A 4 3	♡ Q J	♡ 5
◇ A 6 3 2	◇ Q J 6 3	◇ K Q
♣ 7 6 4	♣ K 8 4 2	♣ Q 8 6 4 2

Using the Rule of 20 would suggest that you should pass (A) since the total of HCP (12) plus the cards in your two longest suits $(4 + 3) = 19$. However, most top players would open (A) with 1NT if playing a weak 1NT or $1\diamondsuit$ otherwise. The reason is that aces are undervalued in the 4-3-2-1 point count. The value of an ace is closer to 4¼ and so (A) is closer to 13 points than 12. This upgrading accounts for the advice in most texts that you should add 1 point if holding all four aces.

The Rule of 20 also suggests that you should open (B) and (C) as both measure 20. You should pass (B) despite its 12 HCP as it has two strikes against it: it is aceless and the Q-J doubleton is a poor holding. Hand (C) should also be passed: it, too, is aceless, the clubs are poor and the doubleton K-Q is poor.

A modification to the Rule of 20 will make your valuation more accurate: Add HCP plus the number of cards in your two longest suits plus the Quick Tricks in the hand.

Quick tricks (QT) are the tricks you figure to win in the first two rounds of a suit. These are tricks you are likely to win whether as declarer or in defence. The quick trick scale is:

A-K = 2   A-Q = 1½   A = 1   K-Q = 1   K = ½ (0 if singleton king)

When counting quick tricks as well, the standard for opening is 22 or more. Hand (A) measures 22, therefore open. Hand B has only 1 QT and measures 21, therefore pass. Likewise, (C) has only 1 QT and its count comes to 21. Therefore pass unless you have some multi-opening to show a weak hand with 5 spades and a second suit.

Tip 2: Add quick tricks to the Rule of 20 to produce the Rule of 22.

3 You are North and dealer, with only East-West vulnerable. What action would you take with this hand?

♠ A Q 9 2
♡ 7
◊ 9 8 7 5 2
♣ A 8 6

This deal arose in the finals of a major Australian event in 2003:

Dealer North : East-West vulnerable

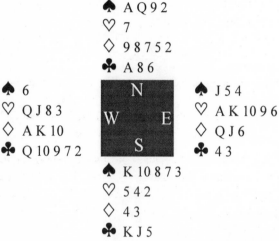

```
                    ♠ A Q 9 2
                    ♡ 7
                    ◊ 9 8 7 5 2
                    ♣ A 8 6
  ♠ 6                                    ♠ J 5 4
  ♡ Q J 8 3          N                   ♡ A K 10 9 6
  ◊ A K 10      W         E              ◊ Q J 6
  ♣ Q 10 9 7 2        S                  ♣ 4 3
                    ♠ K 10 8 7 3
                    ♡ 5 4 2
                    ◊ 4 3
                    ♣ K J 5
```

At most tables North passed and East-West generally had a free run and finished in the unbeatable 4♡. At one table North opened the bidding and North-South went on to reach 4♠ after a competitive auction. This was doubled, but it made when East-West did not find the killing defence. Naturally this was the top result for North-South, but one down would have been just as good compared with the –620 North-South were conceding at the other tables.

Using HCP + two long suits and quick tricks, the North hand measures only 21½, a touch short for the Rule of 22. North's decision to open the bidding was based on this tip:

Tip 3: Reduce the Rule of 22 to 21 at favourable vulnerability.

4 What action would you take as dealer, both sides vulnerable, with the following hands?

(A)	(B)	(C)
♠ A J 10 7 4	♠ A 9 7 4 3	♠ A K J 2
♡ A J 10 3	♡ K	♡ 9 3
◇ 8	◇ A 6 5 2	◇ K 9 8 6
♣ 7 4 3	♣ 8 7 5	♣ 6 4 2

Honour cards in combination are more powerful than honour cards on their own. A holding of Q-J-x opposite three low cards has a strong chance of producing one trick. Q-x-x opposite J-x-x has less of a chance unless you can persuade the opponents to lead the suit, and Q-x-x and J-x-x in one hand opposite x-x-x and x-x-x is weaker still.

It is worth upgrading a hand by ½ a point for the queen or jack in a suit with two higher honours (A-K-Q, A-K-J, A-Q-J, K-Q-J), or J-10 in a suit with one higher honour (suits headed by A-J-10, K-J-10 or Q-J-10). These combinations boost your chances of an extra trick.

On the other hand, honour cards in short suits should be downgraded. K-Q-x opposite x-x-x has potential for two tricks, but K-Q doubleton opposite low cards will make one trick only. Deduct 1 point for a singleton king, queen or jack, and deduct ½ a point for the ace, king, queen or jack in a doubleton suit.

Hand (A) has 10 HCP, 9 for Length, 2 quick tricks: total 21. Being one short of the recommended 22 suggests a pass. Once you upgrade for the two A-J-10 holdings, ½ for each, you reach 22 and should open 1♠.

Hand (B) has 11 (HCP) + 9 (Length) + 2 (QT), total 22. The Rule of 22 indicates an opening bid, but once you deduct 1 for the singleton king, you drop to 21 and should pass, except at favourable vulnerability, where the Rule of 21 is a good guide.

The count for (C) is 21½, but adding ½ for the jack with two higher honours allows you to open. If the jack were elsewhere you would pass.

Tip 4: Upgrade for honours in combination and downgrade for honours in short suits.

5 What action would you take as dealer, both sides vulnerable, with the following hands?

(A)
♠ K J 8 6 3 2
♡ 8
♢ K Q 8 6 2
♣ 5

(B)
♠ Q J 8 6 3 2
♡ A K 7
♢ 6 2
♣ 8 5

(C)
♠ K 9 6 5 3 2
♡ A K 7
♢ 8
♣ 9 6 4

The more shapely a hand, the more attractive it is to open. Where the total for length is eight, your two 'long' suits will be 5-3 or 4-4. If it is 4-4, it is worth adding half a point if your pattern is 4-4-4-1, as this has better playing strength than a 4-4-3-2. Where your total for length is 9, your long suits will be 5-4 or 6-3. Again add ½ if your pattern is 5-4-3-1 or 5-4-4-0 or 6-3-3-1, but not if the residue is 2-2. In other words if your length total is 8 or 9, add ½ for a singleton or a void.

Where your length total is 10 or 11, you are sure to have at least one singleton or a void. With these totals, add ½ only if your hand includes a void.

The count for Hand (A) is 21½. Open with a weak two or a multi-two if your system allows it or open 1♠ at favourable vulnerability. If your values were the same with a 6-2-5-0 or 6-0-5-2 pattern, your count would now be 22 and you should open 1♠ at any vulnerability.

Hand (B) has a count of 21 (10 HCP, 9 for length, 2 quick tricks). Open with a weak 2♠ if available or 1♠ at favourable vulnerability.

Hand (C) has the same high card strength but is worth a 1♠ opening at any vulnerability since the count is 22. You have 10 HCP, 9 for length and 2½ quick tricks. That makes 21½ and you should add ½ for holding a singleton when your length total is 9.

Tips 1-5 reflect the main factors used by top players, not necessarily consciously, in deciding whether to open or not.

Tip 5: When using the Rule of 21 or 22 in deciding whether to open, if your length total is 8 or 9, add ½ for a singleton or a void and if your length total is 10 or 11, add ½ for a void.

6 The auction starts with two passes to you. What action would you take in third seat with these hands?

(A) ♠ 8 7	(B) ♠ 8 7	(C) ♠ J 7 3 2
♡ 9 6	♡ A K Q 5	♡ J 8
◇ K Q J 9 3	◇ 6 5 3 2	◇ 9 7 3 2
♣ Q 9 6 2	♣ 9 6 5	♣ A K Q

With 13 HCP or more you should make your normal opening in third seat. With less strength you should open only if the suit you bid indicates a good lead to partner. If partner can rely on your opening light in third seat only with a decent suit, partner will be quick to lead that suit if the bidding reveals that your opening was underweight. This will be so even if your opening bid was 1♣ or 1◇, suits that do not normally have great lead-directing significance.

Another good test for a third-seat opening is to ask yourself, 'If right-hand opponent would have opened 1♣, would I have wanted to overcall?' If the answer is 'Yes', by all means open in third seat.

In third seat even a strong 4-card major is acceptable for those playing 5-card majors. An excellent guide here is the Suit Quality Test*:
Add the number of cards in the suit you want to bid + the honours in that suit. If the total comes to 7 or more, you should bid that suit in third seat if you are in the 10-12 point range. With fewer points, it would be wise to have a suit quality of at least eight.
(*For more on the Suit Quality Test, see Tip 21 in *100 Winning Bridge Tips*.)

On this basis each of the above hands would be worth a third-seat opening. Hand (A) has only 8 HCP, but the suit quality of the diamonds is eight (five cards + three honours). If partner ends up on lead, a diamond lead cannot do your side damage while other leads might.

With (B), open 1♡, even if you play 5-card majors. The 1♡ bid will score the right lead from partner and may inhibit the opponents from trying a no-trump contract. With (C) open 1♣, the suit you want led, or pass. Do not open that worthless diamond suit.

Tip 6: After two passes be prepared to open any hand which would be a sound overcall at the 1-level, even as low as 8-9 HCP.

7. What action would you take as the dealer, South, with these hands?

(A) Nil vulnerable	(B) Nil vulnerable	(C) E-W vulnerable
♠ K Q 10 9 8 7 5	♠ K Q 10 9 8 7 5	♠ 3 2
♡ 6 4	♡ - - -	♡ 7 6 5
◇ Q 5	◇ Q 5	◇ A K J 10 9 4 2
♣ 9 4	♣ 9 4 3 2	♣ 8

The hand type to open with a pre-empt is a long, strong suit in a hand too weak for a one-opening. Within that framework you may open with a three-bid or a four-bid and, if the suit is a minor, a five-opening is also available. The level chosen depends on the number of playing tricks held and the vulnerability. Not vulnerable a three-opening typically has six playing tricks, or seven losers, while a four-opening is expected to have seven playing tricks or six losers. When vulnerable, an extra playing trick is expected and pre-empts at unfavourable vulnerability should be within about one trick of the contract.

Even so, the shape of the hand can influence your decision. Hand (A) is a run-of-the-mill 3♠ opening. Hand (B) has the same HCP but the shape is much better. If you are happy to open 3♠ with (A) then you owe it to yourself to do more with (B) and open 4♠. The actual deal:

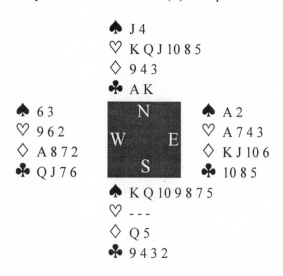

```
              ♠ J 4
              ♡ K Q J 10 8 5
              ◇ 9 4 3
              ♣ A K
    ♠ 6 3          N          ♠ A 2
    ♡ 9 6 2                   ♡ A 7 4 3
    ◇ A 8 7 2   W       E     ◇ K J 10 6
    ♣ Q J 7 6      S          ♣ 10 8 5
              ♠ K Q 10 9 8 7 5
              ♡ - - -
              ◇ Q 5
              ♣ 9 4 3 2
```

Those who opened 3♠ generally played it there for a poor score while those who started with 4♠ made game for a good board. Note that if you give South Hand (A) then 3♠ would be the limit of the hand.

When pre-empting at favourable vulnerability it is a reasonable policy to open with one more than you would at other vulnerabilities. When your suit is a minor you may have a conflict between opening 3♣ or 3♢ to preserve 3NT as an option or opening at the four-level to set the opposition a tougher problem. This deal arose in major event in 2003:

Dealer South : East-West vulnerable

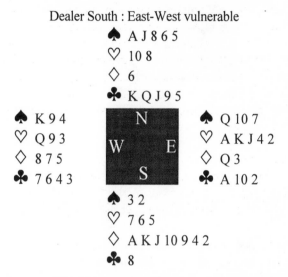

```
              ♠ A J 8 6 5
              ♡ 10 8
              ♢ 6
              ♣ K Q J 9 5
 ♠ K 9 4                      ♠ Q 10 7
 ♡ Q 9 3        N             ♡ A K J 4 2
 ♢ 8 7 5     W     E          ♢ Q 3
 ♣ 7 6 4 3      S             ♣ A 10 2
              ♠ 3 2
              ♡ 7 6 5
              ♢ A K J 10 9 4 2
              ♣ 8
```

No one would quarrel with a 3♢ opening by South with Hand (C). A common scenario was 3♢ : No : No : 3♡, passed out and one down. Australian super-star Tim Seres, en route to winning the event, his 75th national open title, elected to start with 4♢. The bidding went:

WEST	NORTH	EAST	SOUTH
			4♢
No	No	Dble*	No
5♣	Dble	All pass	

*For takeout

West should have passed the double and both East and West were internationals. 4♢ had posed problems which they failed to solve.

In the same event, a dramatic outcome arose on this deal, too, because of the level of pre-emptive opening chosen.

Dealer North : Both vulnerable

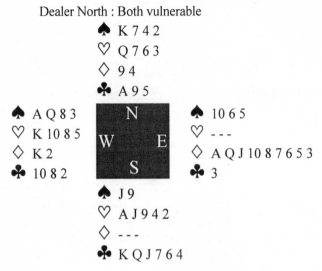

```
            ♠ K 7 4 2
            ♡ Q 7 6 3
            ◇ 9 4
            ♣ A 9 5
♠ A Q 8 3              ♠ 10 6 5
♡ K 10 8 5            ♡ - - -
◇ K 2                 ◇ A Q J 10 8 7 6 5 3
♣ 10 8 2             ♣ 3
            ♠ J 9
            ♡ A J 9 4 2
            ◇ - - -
            ♣ K Q J 7 6 4
```

At one table:

WEST	NORTH	EAST	SOUTH
	No	5◇	All pass

Declarer lost just one spade and one club for +600. You should certainly open 5◇ because of the freakish nature of the hand. To say you have five losers and so just eight playing tricks ignores the power of such a long suit. At another table:

WEST	NORTH	EAST	SOUTH
		4◇	4♡
Double	No	No	No

Declarer had no trouble holding the losers to one spade and two hearts. South's courage in bidding 4♡ and staying there when doubled was well rewarded.

Tip 7: When choosing a pre-empt, be prepared to open at a higher level with freakish shape or at favourable vulnerability.

18

8	WEST	NORTH	EAST	SOUTH
				1♢
	No	1♠	No	1NT*
	No	?		
	*15-17			

What action would you take now as North with these hands?

(A) Both vulnerable
♠ Q 10 8 7
♡ 6 3
♢ Q J 5 2
♣ 7 4 3

(B) Both vulnerable
♠ A 10 9 3
♡ 6 3
♢ Q J 5 2
♣ 7 4 3

When you have a choice between passing 1NT or reverting to opener's minor, choose the minor suit if your point count is likely to be 22 or less, but pass 1NT if the total combined count is likely to be 23-24. It is reasonable to pass 1NT even with a combined 22 if your hand contains some 10s and 9s. On that basis, you should revert to 2♢ with (A) and pass 1NT with (B).

If your side has only 20-21 points, 1NT is not safe and an overtrick is most unlikely. The minor suit part-score is more likely to yield a plus.

When your side has 23-24 points, 1NT is likely to be safe and an overtrick is feasible. With this strength your minor suit contract will probably produce 9 tricks for +110 (10 tricks for +130 is unlikely if your side is below 25-26 points), but 1NT with an overtrick will give you +120 and a better board.

Playing pairs, your aim is to be in the contract that will give you the better score most of the time. It is the frequency of the better outcome that influences your decision. Most of the time, 2♢ will give you a good result when points are evenly shared, more or less, between the two sides. You will score more in 1NT most of the time, but not all of the time, when your side has the preponderance of strength.

Tip 8: At pairs choose a minor suit fit when your combined count is up to 21, but be happy to play in 1NT with 23-24 points together.

9

	WEST	NORTH	EAST	SOUTH
	1♣	No	?	

What action would you take as East with these hands?

(A) ♠ 9 6 3	(B) ♠ A J	(C) ♠ A J 2
♡ K Q 6 4	♡ A 9 6 3	♡ A Q 6 3
◇ Q 7 5 3	◇ K J 7 5	◇ K Q J 5
♣ 7 5	♣ 7 5 2	♣ 7 5

The general rule with 4-card suits is to bid up-the-line. After 1♣ it may be better to hide your diamond suit and show the major first. This applies when you are strong enough to make a no-trump contract likely, generally in the 10-15 points range.

(A) With a weak hand, bid 1◇. If partner has a minimum opening with 5 clubs and 4 diamonds, you may be better off in a diamond part-score.

WEST	EAST	WEST	EAST
♠ 5 4	♠ 9 6 3	1♣	1◇
♡ 8 3	♡ K Q 6 4	2◇	No
◇ A K 6 2	◇ Q 7 5 3		
♣ A J 8 6 2	♣ 7 5		

East-West have reached a sound part-score and are well-placed to push on to 3◇ if North-South compete in spades. What will happen if East responds 1♡? West will rebid 2♣ and play it there. East is not strong enough to take a second bid. 2◇ should make eight tricks for +90 and might make nine tricks for +110. You would be struggling in 2♣ to make eight tricks, while 1NT is likely to fail.

The 1◇ response also allows opener to bid hearts first. When a heart fit exists the stronger hand will be declarer. This can be an advantage when there is a significant disparity in the strengths of the hands.

Players tended to respond 1♡ in the past for fear of an opponent intervening in spades. With the use of competitive doubles (*see* Tip 32) this is no longer a threat. If the bidding starts 1♣ : (No) : 1◇ : (1♠), opener can double for takeout to show a 4-card heart suit.

(B) This time it is better to respond 1♡. Your plan is to play in hearts if opener has support or to rebid 3NT if nothing exciting is revealed by partner's rebid. When slam is unlikely, avoid minor suit games. With no more than game values, focus on major suit fits and 3NT when no major suit fit is feasible.

Concealing your diamond suit may be beneficial if you finish in 3NT. Suppose the bidding goes 1♣ : 1♡, 1♠ : 3NT. What lead are you likely to receive? A diamond lead into your K-J-x-x is likely to be very helpful. If you were anxious for a heart lead, you might respond 1◇:

♠ A J   ♡ K Q 10 7   ◇ J 9 4 3   ♣ Q 8 4

With this collection it might work well to respond 1◇. If the bidding does go 1♣ : 1◇, 1♠ : 3NT, you are likely to receive a heart lead, and that will not hurt at all. You will not miss out on a heart contract by bidding 1◇, as partner can rebid 1♡ over 1◇ if holding four hearts.

(C) This time it is sensible to respond 1◇. You are strong enough for a slam even opposite a minimum opening with diamond support. If you respond 1♡, there is no convenient way to introduce the diamonds later without distorting the shape of your hand.

WEST	EAST
♠ 5 4	♠ A J 2
♡ K 7	♡ A Q 6 3
◇ A 9 6 2	◇ K Q J 5
♣ K Q J 6 3	♣ 7 5

6◇ is an excellent slam and will succeed most of the time. It should be no problem reaching the slam after the bidding starts 1♣ : 1◇, 2◇ ... If no trump fit comes to light and West has shown a minimum opening, East can always subside in 3NT.

Tip 9: After a 1♣ opening, if you have 4 diamonds and a 4-card major, prefer to respond 1◇ if you are in the 6-9 point range or with more than 16 HCP. In the 10-15 point range, bid your major first as long as you have a comfortable no-trump rebid. You might still choose a 1◇ response to try to ward off a diamond lead.

10

	WEST	NORTH	EAST	SOUTH
	1♠	No	?	

What action would you take as East with:

♠ A Q 3 2   ♡ K J 7 4   ◇ 6 4   ♣ Q J 3

If your methods include a forcing raise in spades (such as Jacoby 2NT) that would be the choice of most players. Still, that may not lead to the best pairs contract. With a 5-3 or 5-4 fit in one major and a 4-4 fit in the other major, you will score better most of the time by playing in your 4-4 fit. A-Q-x-x opposite K-J-x-x scores only four tricks if this is a side suit or if you are playing no-trumps. If it is your trump suit, you may be able to generate an extra trick by ruffing in one hand or the other. Put another way, a 4-4 side suit gives you no discards, but a 5-4 fit can give you one discard and a 5-3 fit might give you two.

WEST	EAST	WEST	EAST
♠ K J 8 7 6	♠ A Q 3 2	1♠	2♣
♡ A Q 5 2	♡ K J 7 4	2♡	4♡
◇ A 2	◇ 6 4	No	
♣ 6 5	♣ Q J 3		

If West does not rebid 2♡, East can then show the spade support. Played in spades there are only ten tricks as long as the defenders attack diamonds early enough. In hearts you will usually make eleven tricks.

4♡ will outscore 4♠ whenever hearts are 3-2: 68% of the time.
4♡ and 4♠ score the same when hearts are 4-1: 28% of the time.
4♡ will do worse than 4♠ when hearts are 5-0: 4% of the time.

By locating the 4-4 heart fit, you will achieve a better score 68% of the time and a worse score only 4% of the time. Even though 4♠ is safer, you cannot afford to buck these odds when playing pairs. The practical advice is to beware of supporting one major unless you are sure that a 4-4 fit does not exist in the other major. Even if you have located a fit in one major you may explore the possibility of playing in the other major.

Tip 10: Do not commit to a 5-3 or 5-4 fit in one major if a 4-4 fit is feasible in the other major.

11

	WEST	NORTH	EAST	SOUTH
	1NT*	No	?	
	*12-14			

What action would you take as East with:

(A)	♠ A K 6 4	(B)	♠ A K 6 4	(C)	♠ A K 6 4
	♡ 9 4		♡ K Q		♡ K Q
	◇ A 9 7 2		◇ A 9 7 2		◇ A Q J 2
	♣ Q J 3		♣ Q J 3		♣ Q J 3

With a choice of 3NT or a 4-4 major fit, you are usually better off to play in the major as long as at least one of you has a ruffing value. With (A), use 2♣ Stayman to seek a spade fit. If so, play in 4♠. The major suit game is usually safer than 3NT. When both contracts succeed the major suit game will usually outscore 3NT. Most of the time 4♡ or 4♠ on a 4-4 fit scores one trick more than 3NT.

WEST	EAST	WEST	EAST
♠ Q 10 3 2	♠ A K 8 6	1NT	2♣
♡ A 6 3	♡ 9 4	2♠	4♠
◇ K 8 6 4	◇ A 9 7 2	No	
♣ K 7	♣ Q J 3		

3NT might fail on a heart lead. If hearts are 4-4 and you make 3NT those in 4♠ will probably outscore you. If suits break normally, you will make ten tricks in spades but only nine in no-trumps.

With your partnership strength in the 25-29 point zone, when 3NT makes an overtrick for 430 or 630, you often find that the major suit game also scores an overtrick for 450 or 650.

WEST	EAST (A)	WEST	EAST
♠ A 8 6	♠ Q J 10	1NT	2♣
♡ K Q 9 5	♡ A J 7 2	2♡	4♡
◇ A 7 4 2	◇ 9 6 3	No	
♣ 9 6	♣ A K 2		

In 3NT you will make ten tricks if the ♠K is onside. In 4♡, barring fiendish breaks, you will make eleven tricks with the ♠K onside.

When the partnership has 30-31 points, you have so much strength that most suits are doubly stopped. An unguarded suit is possible but highly unlikely. The chance of a danger suit with just one stopper is low.

WEST	EAST (B)	WEST	EAST
♠ Q 10 3 2	♠ A K 6 4	1NT	4NT
♡ A 6 3	♡ K Q	No	
♢ K 8 6 4	♢ A 9 7 2		
♣ K 7	♣ Q J 3		

Here the partnership has 31 points. Whether you play in spades or in no-trumps, the likely outcome is eleven tricks. With so much strength East should not look for the major suit fit. The 4NT response invites opener to bid on if maximum. With a minimum West passes and the best pairs' spot is reached. If suits break badly, you may be limited to ten tricks or worse in spades, but ten tricks are always there in no-trumps.

WEST	EAST	WEST	EAST
♠ A 8 6 4 2	♠ J 7 3	1♠	2♣
♡ K 5	♡ Q J 10	2NT	4NT
♢ A 9 5	♢ K Q J	No	
♣ K J 4	♣ A Q 7 2		

You have a 5-3 fit in spades, but no-trumps is vastly superior. 4♠ may fail on a 4-1 break, but ten tricks should be no problem in no-trumps. One of the traps in the 30-31 point zone is the weak trump suit.

WEST	EAST (C)	WEST	EAST
♠ Q 10 3 2	♠ A K 6 4	1NT	6NT
♡ A 6 3	♡ K Q	No	
♢ K 8 6 4	♢ A Q J 2		
♣ K 7	♣ Q J 3		

East knows that a grand slam will not be a good bet (West cannot hold all of ♠Q, ♡A, ♢K and ♣A-K). With some vital card missing but enough for a small slam, East bids it in the higher-scoring strain.

Tip 11: With a major suit fit and also a hand reasonably suitable for no-trumps, play in the major suit when your combined count is 25-29, but choose no-trumps when your side has 30 points or more.

24

12   Dealer West : Both vulnerable
              WEST   NORTH   EAST   SOUTH
              ?

Playing 1NT as 12-14, what action would you take as West with:

♠ 6 3 2   ♡ A J 7 6 3   ◇ A 7 4   ♣ K 8

With a 5-3-3-2 pattern it is routine to open 1NT with the right strength when the 5-card suit is a minor. You would sooner reach 3NT than 5-of-a-minor and so opening 1NT takes priority over the minor suit opening.

What if your 5-card suit is a major? Now the issue is not clear-cut, since a major suit game will often outscore 3NT. Views differ whether to open with the major or whether to open 1NT when your strength meets the 1NT requirements. Traditional advice has been to start with the major suit, but there are strong arguments in favour of choosing the 1NT opening.

● If no major suit fit exists, you have disclosed less of your hand.

● If a major suit fit does exist and your bidding starts 1♡ : 2♡ or 1♠ : 2♠, strong opponents will compete. You then have to let them play the hand or compete to the 3-level with minimum values.

● Opening 1NT eliminates many rebid problems that occur after a 1♡ : 1♠ start.

● Opening 1NT allows responder to transfer to 2♡ and play there, which you could not do after a 1♠ opening. A 1♠ opening may lose a heart fit entirely.

● Opening 1NT can keep the bidding lower.

● Opponents are generally more reluctant to compete after a 1NT opening than after a suit opening.

● An opponent may have a natural 2♣ or 2◇ overcall if you open 1♡ or 1♠, but these bids might be conventional after a 1NT opening. .

Consider this deal, with West dealer and both sides vulnerable:

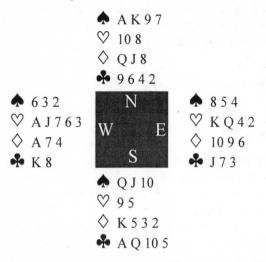

♠ A K 9 7
♡ 10 8
◇ Q J 8
♣ 9 6 4 2

♠ 6 3 2
♡ A J 7 6 3
◇ A 7 4
♣ K 8

♠ 8 5 4
♡ K Q 4 2
◇ 10 9 6
♣ J 7 3

♠ Q J 10
♡ 9 5
◇ K 5 3 2
♣ A Q 10 5

What will happen if West opens 1♡? North should pass. East will raise to 2♡, passed back to North. Of course, North should re-open with a takeout double and North-South should then find their club fit with 3♣, although an aggressive South might choose 2♠. Both of these contracts make easily. If West soldiers on to 3♡, that will be two down for −200 and a hideous score. Even 2♡ cannot make.

What if West opens 1NT. North will pass and so will East. Would you come in against 1NT on the South cards? A convention such as DONT would allow South to bid 2♣, showing clubs and a higher suit. That will find the North-South trump fit. As most pairs do not play DONT and use 2♣ for other purposes, 1NT will be passed out.

If North leads a spade or a diamond, the defence can hold declarer to six tricks. One down, −100, is much better than North-South making nine tricks in spades or clubs. If North decides on a passive club lead, West will make 1NT for a huge score. Despite the 9-card heart fit, West travels better in 1NT.

Tip 12: With a 5-card major and a 5-3-3-2 pattern, opening 1NT with the appropriate strength can be a real winner.

13 If you do decide to allow your partnership to open 1NT when holding a 5-3-3-2 pattern with a 5-card major, it is sensible to give responder a way of discovering whether opener does have a 5-card major. The right game may easily be in the major suit.

WEST	EAST
♠ A J 6 4 2	♠ K 8 3
♡ A 5 2	♡ K J 10 4
◇ 9 6	◇ A 7
♣ K 9 4	♣ Q J 5 2

The best spot for the partnership is 4♠. On a diamond lead you need both majors to behave to succeed in 3NT. Five spades two hearts and one diamond will not be enough. If you are in 4♠, you can afford to lose one spade if you find the ♡Q or if you have five spade tricks, you can afford to lose a heart. Playing in spades you do not mind giving up a trick to the ♣A, which would be almost certainly fatal in 3NT after a diamond lead.

This is a relatively simple structure for 5-Card Major Stayman and does not damage your other bidding after a 1NT opening (such as transfers, jump-responses and so on).

1NT : 2♣
?
2♡ / 2♠ = minimum hand, 5-card suit
3♡ / 3♠ = maximum hand, 5-card suit

It is worthwhile distinguishing the minimum and the maximum openings at once. Responder can then pass 2♡ / 2♠ with invitational values since opener is known to be minimum.

WEST	EAST	WEST	EAST
♠ A J 6 4 2	♠ K 8 3	1NT	2♣
♡ A 5 2	♡ K J 10 4	2♠	4♠
◇ 9 6	◇ A 7	No	
♣ K 9 4	♣ Q J 5 2		

Once opener shows a 5-card major, responder will not need to look for a 4-4 fit. To start with 1NT, opener will not be 5-4 in the majors.

What if opener does not have a 5-card major? Responder may still want to locate a 4-card major. Again it is useful for opener to be able to indicate minimum or maximum at once.

1NT : 2♣
?
2♦ = minimum hand, no 5-card major
2NT = maximum hand, no 5-card major

With enough for game and interested in a 4-4 major fit, responder just repeats the inquiry with 3♣. So, 2♣ = 'Do you have a 5-card major?' If the reply is 'No', then 3♣ = 'Do you have a 4-card major?'

1NT : 2♣	or	**1NT : 2♣**
2♦ : 3♣		2NT : 3♣
?		**?**

Opener can now show a 4-card major. With 4-4 in the majors opener bids 3♡, the cheaper suit, just the same as after 2♣ simple Stayman.

WEST	EAST	WEST	EAST
♠ A J 6 4	♠ K Q 8 3	1NT	2♣
♡ A 5 2	♡ K J 10 4	2♦	3♣
♢ 9 6	♢ A 7	3♠	4♠
♣ K 9 4 3	♣ Q J 5	No	

To locate your 4-4 fit just takes an extra round of bidding.

Where opener rebids 2♦, minimum with no 5-card major, responder should rebid at the two-level with invitational values. Thus 2♡ = four hearts, 2♠ = four spades and 2NT = no 4-card major. With a fit for the major, opener passes 2♡ or 2♠. Without a fit for the major, opener can bid 2♠ (four spades) or 2NT over 2♡, or 2NT over 2♠.

One can play a simpler set of replies to 2♣ (2♡ / 2♠ = 5-card suit, 2♦ = no 5-major), but the extended version above is recommended.

Tip 13: If your partnership allows or encourages a 1NT opening with the right strength and a 5-3-3-2 pattern with a 5-card major, it is sensible to use a 2♣ response to ask for a 5-card major.

14   Dealer West : Both vulnerable

WEST	NORTH	EAST	SOUTH
1NT	No	?	

With 1NT 12-14, what action would you take as East with:

♠ Q J 7 5   ♡ A 6 3   ◇ A K 4   ♣ 8 3 2

Some recommend jumping straight to 3NT because the hand is flat, others would urge you to use 2♣ Stayman since a 4-4 major suit fit might well play better than 3NT.

If you jump to 3NT, you will be in the right spot if the hands are:

WEST	EAST
♠ A K 8 3	♠ Q J 7 5
♡ K Q 5	♡ A 6 3
◇ 9 6 2	◇ A K 4
♣ J 7 6	♣ 8 3 2

Despite the 4-4 spade fit, how can you avoid losing three clubs and one diamond? If you play in 3NT you have nine tricks on top and will succeed most of the time, whenever a club is not led or if clubs are 4-3.

The outcome will not be so rosy if the hands look like this:

WEST	EAST
♠ A K 8 3	♠ Q J 7 5
♡ K Q 5	♡ A 6 3
◇ 9 7 6 2	◇ A K 4
♣ J 6	♣ 8 3 2

Now you want to be in 4♠. 3NT might easily fail on a club lead. Even if 3NT does make, you will make ten tricks in 4♠ most of the time and outscore 3NT. If both hands are 4-3-3-3, 3NT is the spot, but if either opener or responder is 4-4-3-2, the 4-4 major fit is likely to be better. Since a 4-4-3-2 occurs almost three times more often than a 4-3-3-3, if you regularly use Stayman with a 4-3-3-3, you will be right about three times out of four when a 4-4 major fit does exist. To jump to 3NT with a 4-3-3-3 will be right only one time in four if there is a 4-4 major fit.

Wouldn't it be nice if you could be right almost always instead of about 75% of the time. To do that all you need to know is whether opener is 4-3-3-3 or not. Using the 5-Card Major Stayman from Tip 13, one easy step solves this problem:

1NT : 2♣   or   **1NT : 2♣**
2◇ : 3♣   **2NT : 3♣**
?   **?**

3♡ / 3♠ = 4-card major plus a doubleton.
3◇ = some 4-3-3-3 pattern
3NT = no 4-card major and not 4-3-3-3

Using this approach, the problem vanishes:

WEST	EAST	WEST	EAST
♠ A K 8 3	♠ Q J 7 5	1NT	2♣
♡ K Q 5	♡ A 6 3	2◇	3♣
◇ 9 6 2	◇ A K 4	3◇	3NT
♣ J 7 6	♣ 8 3 2	No	

On learning opener is 4-3-3-3, responder ceases inquiries. On the other hand:

WEST	EAST	WEST	EAST
♠ A K 8 3	♠ Q J 7 5	1NT	2♣
♡ K Q 5	♡ A 6 3	2◇	3♣
◇ 9 7 6 2	◇ A K 4	3♠	4♠
♣ J 6	♣ 8 3 2	No	

When 3♠ shows four spades and a 4-4-3-2 pattern, the spade game is chosen. The same contract would be reached here:

WEST	EAST	WEST	EAST
♠ A K 8 3	♠ Q J 7 5	1NT	2♣
♡ K Q 7 5	♡ A 6 3	2◇	3♣
◇ 9 6 2	◇ A K 4	3♡	3NT
♣ J 6	♣ 8 3 2	4♠	No

3♣ asked for a 4-card major and the 3NT rebid denied interest in hearts. As responder must logically have spades, opener bids 4♠.

If responder is the one with the doubleton, a 3♢ 4-3-3-3 pattern with opener will not deter responder from continuing the search:

WEST	EAST	WEST	EAST
♠ A K 8 3	♠ Q J 7 5	1NT	2♣
♡ K Q 5	♡ A 6 3	2♢	3♣
♢ 9 6 2	♢ A K 4 3	3♢	3♠
♣ J 7 6	♣ 8 3	4♠	No

Over 3♢, responder's 3♠ shows four spades and asks for support and opener raises. If opener's 4-card suit were elsewhere, the rebid would be 3NT.

It is well-known that a 4-3-3-3 opposite a 4-3-3-3 will usually be best in no-trumps. That a 5-3-3-2 opposite a 4-3-3-3 is also better in 3NT most of the time is less well-known. Take a look at these hands:

WEST	EAST	WEST	EAST
♠ J 6 5	♠ K Q 8 7 3	1NT	2♡ (1)
♡ K 6 5	♡ A 8 7	2♠	3NT
♢ K Q 7	♢ A 5	4♠	No
♣ A 9 5 2	♣ 8 7 4	(1) Transfer to spades	

After a transfer and 3NT rebid, opener is expected to revert to the major with three or four trumps or to pass 3NT with a doubleton in responder's suit. When opener is 4-3-3-3, the major suit game may be safer but is usually outscored by 3NT. Here you figure to make ten tricks whether you play in 3NT or 4♠. At pairs then, 3NT is the spot.

You can cater for this problem. Use the transfer-and-rebid 3NT sequence when responder is 5-3-3-2. Opener will pass if 4-3-3-3 and support spades with 3-4 trumps and an outside doubleton. If you want opener to support your 5-card major even if opener is 4-3-3-3, start with 1NT : 2♣ and over 2♢ / 2NT bid 3♡ / 3♠.

Tip 14: You will usually score better by playing a 4-3-3-3 opposite a 4-3-3-3 in no-trumps than in your 4-4 fit. A 5-3-3-2 opposite a 4-3-3-3 is often better in no-trumps, too. It is therefore useful to have a method to deal with this problem.

15 What do each of these sequences mean, using 1NT : 2♣ as simple Stayman and playing transfers?

(a) W	E	(b) W	E	(c) W	E	(d) W	E
1NT	2♣	1NT	2♣	1NT	2♣	1NT	2♣
2♡	3♡	2♠	3♠	2♡	3♠	2♠	3♡

In standard methods, (a) and (b) are simple game invitations. Opener is asked to pass if minimum and bid game if maximum.

Auctions (c) and (d) do not have a sensible natural meaning. With a 5-card major and enough for game, responder would use a transfer sequence. What meaning should one then give to these auctions?

A good idea is to use (c) and (d) as game-forcing raises of opener's major, possibly with slam interest. Standard methods lack such a raise. After 3-level other major, opener bids 3NT if 4-3-3-3, cue-bids with any decent hand (including a doubleton) and raises to game otherwise. This approach allows sensible slam exploration at a comfortable level and also solves the problem of the 4-3-3-3 opposite a 4-3-3-3.

WEST	EAST	WEST	EAST
♠ A 3	♠ K Q J	1NT	2♣
♡ A Q 7 2	♡ K J 10 5	2♡	3♠
♢ K J 7 3	♢ A Q	4♢	4♠
♣ 9 5 2	♣ Q J 8 7	No	

4♢ = 1st or 2nd round control in diamonds, no such control in clubs. East now knows slam is not a good bet.

WEST	EAST	WEST	EAST
♠ A 6 3	♠ K 5 2	1NT	2♣
♡ A Q 7 2	♡ K J 10 5	2♡	3♠
♢ K J 7	♢ A Q 3	3NT	No
♣ 9 5 2	♣ J 8 7		

3NT = 4-3-3-3. East can tell that 3NT will usually play better than 4♠.

Tip 15: After 1NT : 2♣, 2♡ or 2♠, responder can use 3-of-the-other-major as a game-force raise to solve several bidding problems.

16   Dealer North : East-West vulnerable

WEST	NORTH	EAST	SOUTH
	1♠	No	1NT
No	2♠	No	?

What would you do now as South with:

♠ Q J   ♡ A 10 6 4   ◇ Q 8 6 3   ♣ 10 6 4

This deal arose in the finals of a national tournament in 2002:

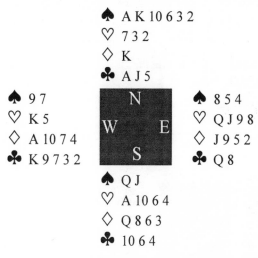

                    ♠ A K 10 6 3 2
                    ♡ 7 3 2
                    ◇ K
                    ♣ A J 5

♠ 9 7		♠ 8 5 4
♡ K 5		♡ Q J 9 8
◇ A 10 7 4		◇ J 9 5 2
♣ K 9 7 3 2		♣ Q 8

                    ♠ Q J
                    ♡ A 10 6 4
                    ◇ Q 8 6 3
                    ♣ 10 6 4

Despite the 15 HCP and the good 6-card suit, a 2♠ rebid is enough for North because of the singleton king. Four pairs played in 4♠ (one after 1♠ : 1NT, 3♠ and the other three when South raised to 3♠). At the other four tables, South passed 2♠. Game failed at three tables but succeeded at one when West ducked the low diamond from dummy and declarer played East for a doubleton honour in clubs.

If South intends to bid on, a marginal decision, 2NT is a better choice. The ♠Q-J opposite North's six spades will be a likely source of tricks. North should raise to 3NT and, as the cards lie, 3NT is unbeatable.

Tip 16: With doubleton support for a 6-card major, consider bidding no-trumps rather than raising the major.

17 Partner opens 2♡, a weak two and next hand passes. What action would you take with these hands:

(A) ♠ A 9 6   (B) ♠ A 9 6   (C) ♠ A 8 5 4 3 2
     ♡ Q J 5 4   ♡ Q J 5 4   ♡ Q 10
     ♢ A 9 4   ♢ A 9 4   ♢ A 8
     ♣ A 7 6   ♣ K Q J   ♣ A 6 5

Suppose you are playing the Ogust Convention where a response of 2NT asks opener for range and suit quality. In reply to your 2NT, opener bids 3♢, showing a minimum weak two with a suit headed by two of the top three honours. What would your next bid be?

In each case you have to decide whether to try 3NT or play in 4♡. This is a possible scenario for (A):

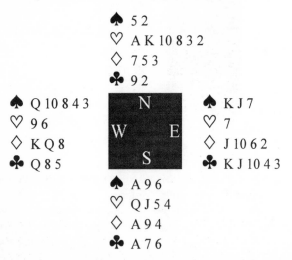

```
                    ♠ 5 2
                    ♡ A K 10 8 3 2
                    ♢ 7 5 3
                    ♣ 9 2
  ♠ Q 10 8 4 3        N        ♠ K J 7
  ♡ 9 6                        ♡ 7
  ♢ K Q 8       W        E     ♢ J 10 6 2
  ♣ Q 8 5            S         ♣ K J 10 4 3
                    ♠ A 9 6
                    ♡ Q J 5 4
                    ♢ A 9 4
                    ♣ A 7 6
```

From opener's 3♢ rebid, you instantly deduce that partner will hold ♡A-K-x-x-x-x and precious little else of value. It is now a matter of counting your tricks. Hand (A) will produce only nine tricks and so you must not bid 4♡. Some might sign off in 3♡, but since the same nine tricks are available in no-trumps, South should rebid 3NT. You know not only that 4♡ will be a very poor chance, but also that 3NT is the right spot despite your ten-card fit in hearts.

You choose 3NT because you have a running suit and instant winners outside. You do not have any extra tricks to be established. With (B) the club winners are not instant and the ♣A will need to be knocked out. If you choose 3NT this time, a spade or a diamond lead may have unpleasant consequences. When you lose the lead to the ♣A, they may cash too many tricks for your liking. Even if you just make 3NT it will be a poor score with 4♡ also making.

With (C), although nine tricks are highly likely in 3NT, choose 4♡. There is potential for more tricks in hearts. Perhaps partner can ruff a diamond in your hand, perhaps the spades can be set up.

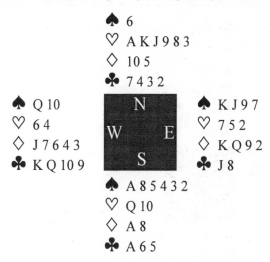

```
                    ♠ 6
                    ♡ A K J 9 8 3
                    ◇ 10 5
                    ♣ 7 4 3 2
   ♠ Q 10          ┌─────────┐      ♠ K J 9 7
   ♡ 6 4           │    N    │      ♡ 7 5 2
   ◇ J 7 6 4 3     │ W     E │      ◇ K Q 9 2
   ♣ K Q 10 9      │    S    │      ♣ J 8
                   └─────────┘
                    ♠ A 8 5 4 3 2
                    ♡ Q 10
                    ◇ A 8
                    ♣ A 6 5
```

Nine tricks in 3NT are easy, but that will be a poor result. As the cards lie there is no diamond ruff, but North can score eleven tricks in 4♡ by careful play, establishing two extra spade winners. Win the diamond lead, cash ♠A, ruff a spade, heart to the ten, ruff a spade, heart to the queen, ruff a spade, draw the last trump, cross to the ♣A and cash the last two spades.

Tip 17: Even with a 6-3 or 6-4 major suit fit, 3NT can be right if you have a running suit and instant winners outside. If you have to set up extra tricks, the major suit game is usually better.

18 Dealer East : East-West vulnerable

WEST	NORTH	EAST	SOUTH
		No	1♡
No	1♠	No	2◇
No	3♣*	No	3◇
No	?		

*Fourth-suit forcing to game

What would you do now as North with:

♠ K Q 10 6   ♡ 10 7 4   ◇ Q 4   ♣ A K 10 6

This deal arose in the semi-finals of a national tournament in 2003:

Half the field played in 4♡ and failed. A diamond lead or a spade lead followed by a diamond switch will beat 4♡ if the defence finds the diamond ruff. On other leads declarer can succeed, but the winning sequence is not straightforward.

The others reached 3NT and made easily. With better than two stoppers in the black suits, 3NT was a sensible choice.

Tip 18: Even with a 5-3 fit in a major suit, 3NT may well be better when you are very strong in partner's short suits.

19   Dealer East : Both vulnerable

East passes. What would you do as South with:

♠ A J 7 6 5 4 2   ♡ Q 5 4   ◇ 6   ♣ 8 5

Your basic choices are 3♠, a weak 2♠ or No Bid. The full deal comes from a national event in 2002:

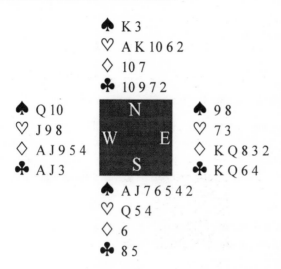

                ♠ K 3
                ♡ A K 10 6 2
                ◇ 10 7
                ♣ 10 9 7 2

♠ Q 10   ♠ 9 8
♡ J 9 8   N   ♡ 7 3
◇ A J 9 5 4   W   E   ◇ K Q 8 3 2
♣ A J 3   S   ♣ K Q 6 4

                ♠ A J 7 6 5 4 2
                ♡ Q 5 4
                ◇ 6
                ♣ 8 5

You could argue in favour of a pass because of the good holding in the other major, but most would want to start with a pre-empt. Concerned about the quality of the spades, I chose a meek 2♠ bid. West doubled, East responded 3◇ and they played it there for +110. Most others opened 3♠, raised to 4♠ by North. That requires no more than avoiding a trump loser and quite a few scored +650.

The 'what-if' syndrome is a dangerous mentality. What if trumps don't break? What if both finesses lose? What if I'm doubled and go three down? The fear of loss is a serious inhibiting factor. Try to eradicate it from your game. (I should listen to my own advice.)

Tip 19: Do not open with a weak two with a decent 7-card suit. Be prepared to take your chances and choose a three-opening or higher, even when you are vulnerable.

20 Most pairs players use transfers after a 1NT opening, especially into the majors. Thus, 1NT : 2♦ = 'I have 5+ hearts' and 1NT : 2♡ = 'I have 5+ spades'. Opener is expected to bid responder's suit next. The primary purpose is not to make opener declarer, though that can be of benefit, but rather to give the partnership more options in responding to 1NT. Where 1NT : 2♡ or 1NT : 2♠ are used as weakness takeouts, the response has one single purpose, to show a weak hand. After a 1NT : 2♦ / 2♡ transfer and 2♡ / 2♠ from opener, responder can pass if weak, bid 2NT as a game-invitation with a 5-card major, raise to the three-level to invite game with a 6-card major, jump to 3NT with a 5-card major to offer a choice of games, jump to 4-major or bid a new suit as a natural bid, forcing to game. Thus your bidding vocabulary has been greatly expanded.

The normal action after a transfer is to bid responder's major. Occasionally your hand will be worth a jump to the three-level in responder's major. To justify this jump ('super-accept') your hand should contain all three of these positive features for partner's suit:
● 4-card support for partner.
● Maximum points rather than minimum. If borderline, upgrade a hand with aces and kings; downgrade one with many jacks and queens.
● A ruffing value via an outside doubleton.

The bidding starts 1NT : 2♡, transfer. What would you do as opener with each of these hands:

(A) ♠ A J 6 4	(B) ♠ A J 6 4	(C) ♠ A J 6 4	(D) ♠ 9 6
♡ Q 7	♡ 7 5	♡ 7 5 3	♡ A K 5
♦ K 9 8 3	♦ K Q 4 2	♦ K Q 4	♦ K Q 4 2
♣ Q J 2	♣ A 10 8	♣ A 10 8	♣ Q 9 8 3

(A) 2♠ is enough. Borderline, but too many queens and jacks.
(B) 3♠. All three positive features are present.
(C) 2♠. You have no ruffing value.
(D) 2♠. You are not permitted to decline the transfer.

Tip 20: If partner transfers to a major after your 1NT opening, accept the transfer at the two-level on most hands. Jump-accept to the three-level only with all three positive features.

21 Partner opens 1NT, 12-14, and second hand passes. What would you respond with each of these hands?

(A) ♠	9 5	(B) ♠	6	(C) ♠	A 4 2
♡	6 3	♡	A 6	♡	8
◇	A K Q 9 7 4	◇	K J 9 6 5	◇	A J 2
♣	K Q 2	♣	A J 6 4 2	♣	K J 10 8 7 4

Since pairs strategy involves not playing in a minor suit game, it is sensible to gamble on 3NT if you have game values, no major suit and no slam ambitions. By all means explore the possibility of a major suit game, but do not suggest a minor suit fit to partner.

Unless you have special responses available, each of the above hands would be worth a jump to 3NT and not a minor suit response. Risky? Of course, but what do you want? Safety or winning? What you do desperately need when you bid 3NT on such hands is a sympathetic partner who will not rebuke you if the gamble does not come off.

Some partnerships have developed ways to overcome such problems (via splinter bids in response to 1NT to show the short suit). Without such methods, jump to 3NT and take your chances.

The same philosophy applies to transfer auctions. Suppose partner opens 1NT. After your 2♡, transfer to spades, opener duly bids 2♠. How would you continue with this hand:

♠ K J 10 6 3   ♡ 9   ◇ A Q 4   ♣ K 6 5 3

If you rebid 3♣, this will show 5+ spades and 4+ clubs and is forcing to game. The trouble is that is also suggests slam values. If you are prepared to play in 5♣ opposite a minimum, you must be close to 6♣ opposite a maximum. A raise by partner to 4♣ will put you beyond the likely best spot of 3NT.

With such hands, transfer to your major and continue with 3NT. That gives partner the choice of 3NT or the major suit game. The same philosophy applies after a 2NT opening and a transfer to a major.

Tip 21: After a 1NT or 2NT opening, do not introduce a minor suit into a game-forcing auction unless you have slam ambitions.

22 Partner opens 1♠ and second hand passes. What would you respond with each of these hands?

(A) ♠ K 8 7 4 (B) ♠ A 5 3 (C) ♠ 8 6 4 3 (D) ♠ J 6 5
  ♡ K 9 3   ♡ J 7   ♡ K Q J   ♡ J 10 4 2
  ◇ 9 7 6   ◇ J 8 6 3   ◇ 9 5 4   ◇ K 8 6 3
  ♣ 8 5 2   ♣ 8 7 5 4   ♣ 7 4 2   ♣ J 5

Each of these hands has enough points to warrant a raise to 2♠, whether you are playing 5-card majors or 4-card suits, but a 1NT response will provide a better result most of the time. Each of these hands has ten losers (the loser count looks only at the top three cards in each suit and anything below the queen is a loser). Responding 1NT certainly runs a risk – you may be left to play in 1NT – but to raise to 2♠ runs an even greater risk. If partner plays you for the normal 6-9 points and 8-9 losers for a raise to the two-level, partner may take further action and you are probably headed for a minus score.

After a raise to 2♠ partner is eager to take action. The raise spurs partner on. If the opponents compete, partner will probably compete above them at the 3-level. This is also likely to produce a negative result because your hand is so short of tricks.

If you respond 1NT a number of good things can happen. If left to play in 1NT, you may achieve a respectable score. Perhaps you make 1NT when 2♠ would have failed. Even if you go minus, perhaps 1NT fails by fewer tricks than 2♠ (or 3♠) would. Perhaps your 1NT inhibits competition and they could have made a part-score, which would gain them more than your loss in 1NT.

If partner does not pass 1NT, partner may rebid in another suit and you might locate a better fit. On (D) for example, if opener rebids 2♡ you have certainly done better than if you had raised to 2♠.

If partner rebids in another suit and your preference is for spades, simply revert to 2♠. That will not sound nearly as encouraging as an immediate raise to 2♠. This sequence has a huge advantage. Your preference sounds reluctant and you may not have genuine support for spades at all.

As your preference to spades might be on no more than a doubleton, the opponents are now less likely to compete for the part-score and you may buy the contract in 2♠. While 1♠ : 2♠ invites competition, it is much less attractive to compete against an auction which goes, say, 1♠ : 1NT, 2♢ : 2♠.

Another plus for the 1NT response arises when opener rebids the major. After 1♠ : 1NT, 2♠ you would pass on each of the hands opposite and again you are quite likely to buy the contract in 2♠. There is no inkling on this sequence that you have a strong trump fit. It could easily be a 6-1 fit. Opponents who are not strong enough to compete on the first round of bidding are far less likely to come in after 1♠ : 1NT, 2♠, Pass, Pass than after 1♠ : 2♠, Pass, Pass.

Those who use the '1NT Forcing' response have been using this approach for years, raising the major with sound values and taking a delayed raise on the 10-loser or worse hands by replying 1NT first. Those of us who do not fancy the 1NT-Forcing gadget can still adopt the same strategy.

Of course, you may suffer occasional losses by responding 1NT in this situation, but in the long run the upside results will significantly outweigh the downside potential.

Tip 22: If partner opens 1♡ or 1♠ and you have support, but a balanced hand with ten losers, choose a 1NT response rather than a raise to 2♡ / 2♠.

23　　　　Dealer West : Both vulnerable

WEST	NORTH	EAST	SOUTH
1♣	No	1♡	No
2♣	No	?	

What would you do as East with:

♠ 3 2　♡ A 10 9 6 4　♢ A 8 7 2　♣ Q 5

You have the values to invite game but lack a spade stopper for 2NT. With only five hearts, a jump to 3♡ is not satisfactory. The basic choice comes down to 2♢ or 3♣. This is how the auction went in a national tournament:

WEST	EAST	WEST	EAST
♠ A K 9	♠ 3 2	1♣	1♡
♡ 3 2	♡ A 10 9 6 4	2♣	2♢
♢ Q 5	♢ A 8 7 2	2NT	3NT
♣ K 9 8 6 3 2	♣ Q 5	No	

This proved spectacularly unsuccessful (– 400) when repeated spade leads cut West off before the clubs could be set up. A contract of 3♣ would have been successful.

East felt that the ♣Q would solidify West's suit and once West bid 2NT East felt obliged to bid 3NT. He could visualize nine easy tricks opposite something like:

♠ A 9 4　♡ 3 2　♢ 6 5　♣ A K J 6 3 2

For his part, West felt he could not deny the strong spade holding, as the East hand was unlimited. For the forcing 2♢, East might have been much stronger and the club suit need not be the source of tricks. Perhaps the spade stopper was all that East needed for 3NT.

A raise to 3♣ by East would have solved this problem. West would be aware of the club support and could look for 3NT with the right hand. On the actual hand, West has an easy pass of 3♣.

Tip 23: Avoid a forcing bid with invitational values if a descriptive invitational bid is available.

24   Dealer West : Both vulnerable
| WEST | NORTH | EAST | SOUTH |
| 1♡ | No | ? | |

What would you do as East with:

♠ A 8   ♡ Q 10 6 5   ◇ J 8 6 4 3 2   ♣ 5

When your side is known to have ten trumps, it is sound competitive technique to compete for ten tricks. With a weak hand it will usually pay you to bid to game as quickly as possible. The same strategy works when you have a certain or probable 9-card fit and one of the hands has ten cards in two suits. Here East's best action is to jump to 4♡. East has ten cards in two suits and a 9-card fit is certain if East-West play 5-card majors and highly likely even if they play 4-card suits.

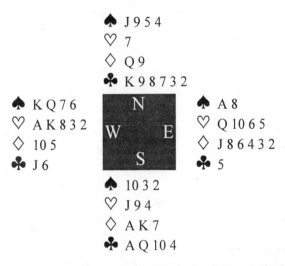

East-West make 4♡ easily and if North-South find 5♣, East-West will score poorly for +500 and much worse if they push on to 5♡. You want to avoid competition on a hand like East's and jumping to game makes it as difficult as possible for North-South to find their spot.

Tip 24: With a 9-card trump fit and 10+ cards in two suits, jump to game at once if you have a weak responding hand.

25 How do you think these hands should be bid? West is the dealer.

WEST	EAST	WEST	EAST
♠ A Q J 7 6 2	♠ K 9 8 4	1♠	?
♡ 3	♡ A 10 9 2		
◇ 9 8 7	◇ - - -		
♣ K Q 5	♣ A 7 6 3 2		

A popular treatment among top players is a double-jump response in a new suit as a 'splinter', showing a shortage (singleton or void) in the suit bid, enough points for game and four or more trumps. On that basis East would respond 4◇. With no high cards in the short suit West would be keen to look for a slam but how to continue?

If West bids 4NT, Roman-Key Card Blackwood (RKCB), East will show three key cards, but unless you have very sophisticated methods, you will not be able to locate the void with East. That would be a pity with 7♠ such a great spot.

Some pairs use methods which can distinguish singleton splinters from void splinters, but it is possible to have the splinter ambiguous and still determine whether it is a void or not and locate key cards.

Using 'scroll', a method devised by Australian champion George Smolanko, the cheapest non-trump bid after a splinter asks about the nature of the shortage. In reply, Step 1 (the cheapest bid) = 'It is a singleton.' Steps 2-5, the next four bids, indicate the shortage is a void and simultaneously show key cards.

After 1♠ : 4◇ above, 4♡ by West = 'scroll'. The replies would mean:

4♠ = singleton diamond
4NT = void diamond and 0 or 3 key cards
5♣ = void diamond and 1 or 4 key cards
5◇ = void diamond and 2 key cards, no trump queen
5♡ = void diamond and 2 key cards, plus the queen of trumps

Using this approach, East's reply to the 4♡ 'scroll' on the hand above would be 4NT, showing a void in diamonds and clearly three key cards, not zero. That would be enough for West to jump to 7♠.

In reply to 4NT RKCB some pairs play 5♣ as 1 or 4 key cards and 5♢ as 0 or 3. Such pairs might also wish to interchange the '0 or 3' and '1 or 4' steps if they adopt 'scroll'.

After the first step showing a singleton, the cheapest bid other than the agreed suit is RKCB. Suppose the hands looked like this:

WEST	EAST	
♠ A Q J 7 6 2	♠ K 9 8 4	East is still worth a jump to
♡ 3	♡ K Q 10 2	4♢, but you would not want
♢ 9 8 7	♢ J	to reach 6♠ this time. How
♣ K Q 5	♣ A 7 6 3	should the bidding go?

WEST	EAST	
1♠	4♢	4♡ = 'scroll'
4♡	4♠	4♠ = singleton diamond
4NT	5♡	4NT = RKCB anyway
5♠	No	5♡ = 2 key cards, no ♠Q

If East had the void, the partnership would reach 6♠:

WEST	EAST	WEST	EAST
♠ A Q J 7 6 2	♠ K 9 8 4	1♠	4♢
♡ 3	♡ K Q 10 2	4♡	5♢
♢ 9 8 7	♢ - - -	6♠	No
♣ K Q 5	♣ A 7 6 3 2		

5♢ = void in diamonds and 2 key cards, no ♠Q.

If you decide to adopt 'scroll' a sensible rule is that 3NT is never 'scroll', but shows a desire to play in 3NT. This is particularly so if opener's suit is a minor. A bid of the agreed suit is also a sign-off, not 'scroll'. Partner can still bid on if very strong and in doing so would use the scroll steps. Thus 1♠ : 4♣, 4♠ : 4NT would show a big hand with a club singleton (over which opener's 5♣ = RKCB) and 5♣ / 5♢ / 5♡ / 5♠ = key cards with a club void.

Tip 25: After a splinter bid by either partner, the scroll method is useful in distinguishing singletons and voids and locating key cards.

Part 2: COMPETITIVE BIDDING

In no other area of match-pointed pairs are the rewards so great for a sound and courageous approach. Time and time again you will find that the winners are not those who can bid to a fine grand slam missed by the field or those who can play an exotic squeeze. No, the winners come from those who are able to judge the right time to push higher, the right time to defend, how high to go, when to double.

Judgement here brings in the match-points, but so does a sound systemic strategy for pairs play. Many find it difficult to throw off the shackles of rubber bridge in this area. Many remain wedded (or welded) to the penalty double. At low levels particularly, the frequency and usefulness of takeout doubles relegates the penalty double to the dinosaur era in the evolution of competitive bidding.

Competitive doubles do not mean that penalties cannot be collected, but they do entail the recognition that takeout doubles have far greater flexibility and usefulness. At pairs, frequency of success counts, not the size of the score. When that factor is accepted, the partnership will adopt low-level takeout doubles in countless areas previously the domain of the penalty double.

Basic strategy for contesting the part-score include the following:

● Pushing from the 2-level to the 3-level when they have bid and raised a suit to the 2-level and then subsided.

● Competing to the 3-level when your side has a trump fit and their auction has stopped at the 2-level in a suit above your trump suit.

● Competing above them at the 3-level only when your side has at least nine trumps or some other significant additional feature.

● Not competing to the 4-level with only part-score values.

The following tips for competitive auctions will supplement your basic strategy.

26

WEST	NORTH	EAST	SOUTH
1♠	No	1NT	2♣
?			

What would you do now as West with:

♠ A 10 9 8 4   ♡ A K 7   ◇ J 7 4 3   ♣ 3

The full deal from a world championship in the 1950s looked like this:

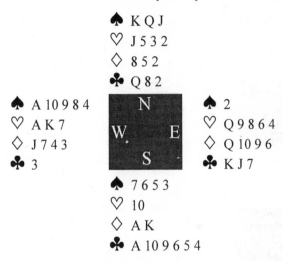

```
                    ♠ K Q J
                    ♡ J 5 3 2
                    ◇ 8 5 2
                    ♣ Q 8 2
    ♠ A 10 9 8 4         N          ♠ 2
    ♡ A K 7                         ♡ Q 9 8 6 4
    ◇ J 7 4 3       W         E     ◇ Q 10 9 6
    ♣ 3                  S          ♣ K J 7
                    ♠ 7 6 5 3
                    ♡ 10
                    ◇ A K
                    ♣ A 10 9 6 5 4
```

At the table West passed 2♣ and so did East. South made ten tricks. At the other table South did not bid and East-West made 3◇.

Today no one would pass with the South cards. Over 2♣, West should double, a competitive double showing a shortage in clubs and a desire to compete. This double does not promise extra strength, merely shortage in the opposition suit and support for the unbid suits. This allows the heart fit to be found, a difficult task if South fails to bid. In reply to the double, East is worth 3♡, which West would pass.

With a hand suitable for penalties, West would pass 2♣, hoping for East to make a takeout double, which West would pass for penalties.

Tip 26: Adopt a style where any double at the 1-level or 2-level of a suit bid is primarily for takeout.

27 How would you treat West's double in this auction?

WEST	NORTH	EAST	SOUTH
1♡	Dble	Rdble	2♣
Dble . . .			

Although you and partner have agreed that, as a general rule, double of a suit bid at the 1-level or 2-level is for takeout (Tip 26), you may wish to specify some situations where such a double is for penalties. This is not a matter of right or wrong, just a matter of agreement. You can choose the above double to be for takeout or for penalties.

Here is a possible list of penalty situations, which can be easily remember by the mnemonic T-R-A-P-P-E-R-S:

T = Third double is always for penalties

R = Redouble and later double = penalties

A = Artificial bid. Doubling that is for penalties, lead-directing.

P = Pre-empt by partner, such as a weak two. Quite a useful rule is that any double after a two-opening is for penalties.

P = Previous penalty pass. Once a double is for penalties or partner has passed for penalties, all future doubles are for penalties.

E = Expose a psyche. After 1♣ : Double or 1♢ : Double, quite a few players bid 1♡ or 1♠ as a psyche. It is sensible to play the double of a major suit bid here as a penalty double.

R = Raise by our side, later doubles = penalties

S = Subsequent double after previous pass of the same suit = penalties

WEST	NORTH	EAST	SOUTH
1♡	2♣	No	No
2♢	3♣	Dble . . .	

East could have doubled 2♣ as a negative double. The pass of 2♣ makes the double of 3♣ penalties.

You may wish to add other situations or delete some of the above, just so long as you and partner have agreements as to which doubles are for takeout and which for penalties.

Tip 27: It is useful to have a list of situations where doubles are for penalties and all other doubles are then played for takeout.

28   Dealer West : Both vulnerable

WEST	NORTH	EAST	SOUTH
1♢	No	1♠	No
2♣	No	2♢	?

What would you do as South with:

♠ A 4 3   ♡ A K 8 7 3   ♢ 8 2   ♣ 10 8 6

On the actual deal North-South paid the price for ineffectual competitive spirit and West did well as declarer:

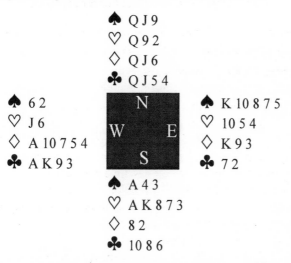

```
                    ♠ Q J 9
                    ♡ Q 9 2
                    ♢ Q J 6
                    ♣ Q J 5 4
   ♠ 6 2                              ♠ K 10 8 7 5
   ♡ J 6                              ♡ 10 5 4
   ♢ A 10 7 5 4                       ♢ K 9 3
   ♣ A K 9 3                          ♣ 7 2
                    ♠ A 4 3
                    ♡ A K 8 7 3
                    ♢ 8 2
                    ♣ 10 8 6
```

South passed and 2♢ was passed out. North led the ♡2. West ruffed the third heart and played a spade: queen – king – ace. West took the club return and played another spade, won by the jack. The rest was easy. West won the next club, cashed ♢A and ♢K and ran the spades. North could ruff the fourth spade, but declarer had the rest for +90.

South should bid 2♡ over 2♠. Risky, yes, but the pass is not free of risk. South can make 2♡ against any defence and the best that East-West can then do is push to 3♢ for one down.

Tip 28: When opener has bid two suits and responder's rebid is preference to the first suit at the 2-level, bid in the direct seat as though you were in fourth seat after two passes.

29   Dealer West : Both vulnerable

WEST	NORTH	EAST	SOUTH
1♦	1♠	Dble	No
2♣	No	?	

What would you do now as East with each of these hands?

(A)	(B)	(C)	(D)
♠ K 7 5	♠ 10 7	♠ 3 2	♠ 7 6 2
♡ J 7 3 2	♡ A 8 5 2	♡ K J 6 3	♡ A 8 6 2
♦ A 6 4	♦ J 4 3	♦ A J 6 5	♦ K 8 7
♣ K 8 7	♣ A Q 8 2	♣ Q 9 6	♣ K J 4

East's negative double of 1♠ promises 4+ hearts and 6+ points. The strength is wide-ranging if East has exactly four hearts. With 5+ hearts, the double denies a hand strong enough for a 2♡ response.

With a weak hand, 6-9 points, East will make a weak rebid, usually passing 2♣ or preference to 2♦. With 10-12 points, you must do more, such as 2NT or raising one of opener's suits to the 3-level.

(A) Bid 2NT. Shows 10-12 points and a stopper in spades. Allows opener to pass, raise to 3NT or revert to a minor.

(B) Raise to 3♣. Shows 10-12 points and club support. Implies no stopper in spades, else a 2NT rebid would be preferable.

(C) Bid 3♦. Shows 10-12 points and diamond support and, as for (B), implies no spade stopper.

(D) Bid 3♦. Not very attractive, but better than any other choice. Much too strong for 2♦ and 2NT is unsuitable with no spade cover.

WEST	EAST	W	N	E	S
♠ 8 2	♠ K 5 3	1♣	1♠	Dble	No
♡ A 3	♡ K Q 9 6	2♣	No	2NT	No
♦ Q 7 2	♦ K 8 4	3♣*	No	No	No
♣ K Q J 9 6 5	♣ 7 4 2	*Choosing the normal part-score			

Tip 29: The hand pattern for a negative double with 10-12 points is normally 4-4-3-2 or 4-3-3-3, occasionally 4-4-4-1. With these values invite game with your rebid even if opener has a minimum opening.

30   Dealer East : Both vulnerable

WEST	NORTH	EAST	SOUTH
		No	1♣
?			

What action would you take as West with:

♠ A J 6 2   ♡ A 10 8   ◇ 10 7 3   ♣ Q J 6

Partner is a passed hand, your shape is terrible and you are vulnerable. Despite your 12 HCP the recommended advice is to pass, but if you are playing against weak opponents you should definitely double. Strong players compete, weak ones do not.

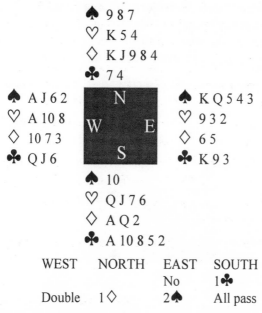

```
              ♠ 9 8 7
              ♡ K 5 4
              ◇ K J 9 8 4
              ♣ 7 4
♠ A J 6 2                      ♠ K Q 5 4 3
♡ A 10 8         N            ♡ 9 3 2
◇ 10 7 3    W        E        ◇ 6 5
♣ Q J 6          S            ♣ K 9 3
              ♠ 10
              ♡ Q J 7 6
              ◇ A Q 2
              ♣ A 10 8 5 2
```

WEST	NORTH	EAST	SOUTH
		No	1♣
Double	1◇	2♠	All pass

As North-South can make ten tricks in diamonds this was a weak effort by them, especially as East had no trouble making 2♠. South should make a takeout double of 2♠, but the timid are afraid of competing. Do not be afraid to exploit this weakness.

Tip 30: Lighten up your requirements for entering the bidding when playing against weak opposition.

Dealer South : Nil vulnerable

WEST	NORTH	EAST	SOUTH
			1♣ (1)
2◇ (2)	Dble (3)	3◇	?

(1) Playing a 15-17 1NT
(2) Weak jump-overcall
(3) Negative double, promises both majors

What would you do as South with:

♠ K J 9 6   ♡ A 10 7   ◇ J 3   ♣ K Q 5 2

When partner has made a negative double, opener's action at the two-level does not show extra strength, even if RHO has bid. For opener to bid at the 3-level when responder has not promised more than 6-9 points, you can expect opener to have around 15-18 points. With less strength opener should pass. Responder can compete further with suitable values, possibly by making another takeout double.

This deal from the USA illustrates a common error in this area:

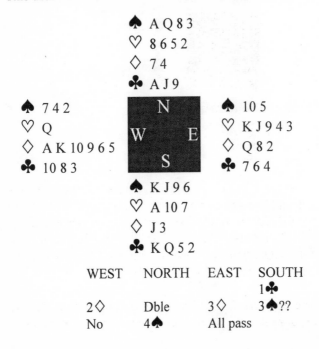

```
                    ♠ A Q 8 3
                    ♡ 8 6 5 2
                    ◇ 7 4
                    ♣ A J 9
  ♠ 7 4 2                          ♠ 10 5
  ♡ Q               N              ♡ K J 9 4 3
  ◇ A K 10 9 6 5  W   E            ◇ Q 8 2
  ♣ 10 8 3          S              ♣ 7 6 4
                    ♠ K J 9 6
                    ♡ A 10 7
                    ◇ J 3
                    ♣ K Q 5 2
```

WEST	NORTH	EAST	SOUTH
			1♣
2◇	Dble	3◇	3♠??
No	4♠	All pass	

This foolish game has two losers in each red suit. You cannot blame North. South should have been much better for the 3♠ bid, at least 15 useful points. South should pass 3♢ and North would compete with a second double, still for takeout. This second double implies 10+ points. With most 6-9 point hands North would pass 3♢. In reply to the second double, South's best action is to pass and collect 300. If South does bid, 3♠ is enough and the silly 4♠ will be avoided.

The play in 4♠ was a contest in missed opportunities. West cashed two diamonds and switched to a trump. (Shifting to the ♡Q is not difficult. Where else would East-West find tricks?) Declarer drew trumps, East pitching a heart and cashed four rounds of clubs, East pitching another heart. The position now was:

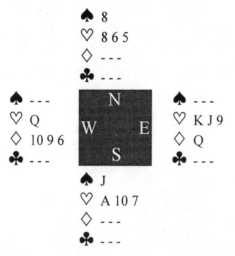

```
              ♠ 8
              ♡ 8 6 5
              ♢ - - -
              ♣ - - -

  ♠ - - -                   ♠ - - -
  ♡ Q          N            ♡ K J 9
  ♢ 10 9 6   W   E          ♢ Q
  ♣ - - -      S            ♣ - - -

              ♠ J
              ♡ A 10 7
              ♢ - - -
              ♣ - - -
```

Declarer now led the ♡7 to West's queen. If East ducked this, the forced ruff-and-sluff would see South home. East overtook with the ♡K and returned the ♡9. Declarer should have succeeded by finessing the ♡10, but rose with the ♡A and was one off. If West had started with ♡Q-J bare, why would East need to overtake? At least justice was served for that awful 3♠ overbid.

Tip 31: After a negative double by responder, opener should not compete to the 3-level in the direct seat with just minimum values.

32 Test yourself on these problems:

(1)   Dealer West : Both vulnerable

WEST	NORTH	EAST	SOUTH
1♥	2♦	No	No
?			

What action should West take with:

♠ A 7 6 ♡ A K 9 6 4 2 ♢ 7 ♣ Q J 4

(2)   Dealer North : Nil vulnerable

WEST	NORTH	EAST	SOUTH
	No	No	1♠
Dble	2♠	No	No
?			

What would you do as West with:

♠ 6 2 ♡ K 9 8 5 ♢ A K J 7 6 2 ♣ A

(3)   Dealer North : Nil vulnerable

WEST	NORTH	EAST	SOUTH
	No	No	1♠
Dble	2♦	No	No
2♥	2♠	No	No
?			

What action would you take as West take with:

♠ A 7 6 ♡ A K 9 6 4 2 ♢ 7 ♣ Q J 4

(1) Many players would re-open with 2♡. This is putting all your eggs in one basket. Yes, the hearts are strong, but the best trump suit is the one where the partnership has the most cards, not your personal best. 2♡ could be right, but partner might hold one of these hands:

(A)	(B)	(C)
♠ Q 9 8 4 2	♠ 8 5 2	♠ K 5 4
♡ 7	♡ 7	♡ 7
♢ 8 6 5 2	♢ J 10 2	♢ K Q 9 6 2
♣ K 5 3	♣ K 10 7 5 3 2	♣ 9 7 5 2

The best action is to double for takeout. If you bid 2♡, partner is likely to pass each time. Partner might try 2NT with (C), yet the best spot is 2♠ on (A), 3♣ on (B) and 2◇ doubled on (C). How will you reach any of these other than by doubling?

(2) Many players would be seduced by the suit texture into a 3◇ bid and that could be right, but 3◇ might also miss the optimal contract. If you bid 3◇, what do you expect partner to do with:

♠ J97 ♡ Q10763 ◇ 54 ♣ J86

Partner will pass 3◇ because the sequence you have chosen, double followed by a new suit, implies a one-suited hand, a hand too strong for an immediate overcall. That is how you would bid if you held:

♠ A6 ♡ 94 ◇ AKJ762 ♣ KQ3

The solution is that West should double 2♠. If partner bids 3♡, fine. If the reply is 3♣, then and only then should you bid 3◇.

(3) West should double 2♠. Partner has heard the auction, has heard you bid 2♡, has heard the opponents bid spades and diamonds and so should be able to make a sensible decision. There is no reasonable interpretation for your double other than you want partner to take action because you are uncertain as to the best action.

The deal arose in the 1989 European Championships and the double eluded the competitors. If you passed 2♠, you have done better than they did, for the opponents are languishing in a 4-2 fit. If you double you have done even better. Partner with six trumps will know what to do and pass for penalties, even though your double is for takeout. It would be remarkable if North-South could then salvage the situation and land in 3♣, their best spot.

If you decided to bid 3♣ or 3♡, you will have to play brilliantly to achieve a plus score. On Viewgraph, the actual West rescued North-South from 2♠ (which was cold for East-West) into 3♣ (which was cold for North-South). Competitive doubles, anyone?

Tip 32: Do not put all your eggs in one basket. Use competitive doubles freely to maximise your options.

33   Dealer West : North-South vulnerable

WEST	NORTH	EAST	SOUTH
1NT (1)	No	2♡ (2)	No
2♠	No	No	?

(1) 12-14   (2) Transfer to spades

What would you do as South with:

♠ 10 7 5   ♡ A 7   ◇ A K J 7 6   ♣ 8 6 2

After a 1NT opening and a transfer bid, passed by responder, be very eager to compete, using double for takeout and 2NT for the minors. Here, bid 3◇. With no second suit, a takeout call is unsuitable. What you need is courage. The deal arose in the 1989 Far East Pairs:

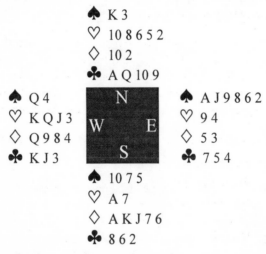

```
                    ♠ K 3
                    ♡ 10 8 6 5 2
                    ◇ 10 2
                    ♣ A Q 10 9
  ♠ Q 4                          ♠ A J 9 8 6 2
  ♡ K Q J 3          N           ♡ 9 4
  ◇ Q 9 8 4      W       E       ◇ 5 3
  ♣ K J 3            S           ♣ 7 5 4
                    ♠ 10 7 5
                    ♡ A 7
                    ◇ A K J 7 6
                    ♣ 8 6 2
```

Even though good defence can set 2♠ by two tricks, declarer made 3◇ by careful play. South took the ♡K lead and played a spade to the king and ace. East switched to a trump, taken by the ace. A heart went to West's jack and West continued with the ◇Q, as good as anything. South won and led a club to dummy's ten. When that held, a heart was ruffed and another club went to the jack and queen. A fourth heart was ruffed and the ♣A cashed. Declarer thus made one heart, five diamonds and three clubs for +110 and a great score.

Tip 33: Compete freely in fourth seat after a transfer bid is passed.

34   Dealer West : Both vulnerable

WEST	NORTH	EAST	SOUTH
1♡	2♢	?	

What would you do as East with:

♠ A 10 9 5 3 2   ♡ Q 2   ♢ 5 2   ♣ K 5 3

Your basic choices are 2♠ or double. The 2♠ bid shows 10+ points and a 5+ suit. You have only 9 HCP, but the suit is six cards long and the queen in opener's suit should be a plus value. The negative double promises only 6 HCP at the 2-level and with a 5+ suit, the range for the double is 6-9 HCP. Essentially you are minimum for a 2♠ response and maximum for a negative double.

It is usually better to take the more conservative action when there is no certainty yet of a trump fit. This is particularly so when playing pairs. The double may let you out at 2♠, your rebid if partner rebids 2♡, although passing 2♡ would not be a criminal offence. If you bid 2♠, that is forcing and you may not able to escape cheaply any more.

These were the East-West hands in a national tournament in 2003:

WEST	EAST	W	N	E	S
♠ - - -	♠ A 10 9 5 3 2	1♡	2♢	2♠	No
♡ A 9 8 7 5	♡ Q 2	3♣	No	3♢	No
♢ K J 4 3	♢ 5 2	3NT	No	No	Dble
♣ A 8 6 2	♣ K 5 3	No	No	No	

Having bid 2♠, East could not tell West's strength for the 3♣ rebid. East should have rebid 3♠, but that would not have met a happy fate either. 3NT doubled was –500 for an horrendous score.

Suppose East had doubled 2♢. West could sensibly pass for penalties, a little speculative, but the shortage in spades makes the pass attractive, and North-South would have been the ones shelling out.

Tip 34: In competitive auctions also, avoid a forcing bid if a cheaper, invitational action is available (see also Tip 23).

35　　　Dealer North : Both vulnerable

WEST	NORTH	EAST	SOUTH
	No	No	1♥
Dble	2♥	?	

What would you do as East with:

♠ 8 6　♥ Q J 2　◇ Q 8 5 2　♣ K J 5 3

When third player bids after partner's takeout double, you are no longer obliged to bid. Then again, you are not forced to pass either. Normally you would pass with 0-5 points, bid an available suit with 6-9 points, bid 2NT (natural, balanced) or jump to the 3-level with 10-12 points and bid game or the enemy suit (to force to game) with 13 points or more.

When you have a choice of major vs minor, bid your major. In the above auction your #1 choice would be spades with a 4+ suit. With equal length suits of the same rank, you can double for takeout, called a responsive double in this auction, asking partner to choose the better suit. After 1♣ / 1◇ : Double : 2♣ / 2◇, Double shows both majors. After 1♥ / 1♠ : Double : 2♥ / 2♠ : Double asks partner to choose a minor suit. Otherwise you have to guess whether to bid 3♣ or 3◇. If you did that, it is possible that you might finish in a 4-3 fit instead of a 5-4 fit. A responsive double involves partner in the decision. The doubler will play a responsive double at the two-level to show about 6-9 points. If stronger, the responsive doubler can bid more later.

WEST	EAST	W	N	E	S
♠ K Q 7 3	♠ 8 6		No	No	1♥
♥ 5	♥ Q J 2	Dble	2♥	Dble	No
◇ K 9 7 6 3	◇ Q 8 5 2	3◇	No	No	No
♣ A 8 6	♣ K J 5 3				

If North or South did compete to 3♥, you would be happy to defend.

Tip 35: After partner's double of a suit opening and a third-hand raise of that suit, double by fourth hand is 'responsive', showing two suits of about equal length and opposite rank to the suit opened.

36   Dealer West : Nil vulnerable

WEST	NORTH	EAST	SOUTH
1♢	No	1♠	2♡
?			

What would you do as West with:

(A)	(B)	(C)
♠ Q J 7 3	♠ Q J 7	♠ J 7
♡ 7 4 2	♡ 7 4 2	♡ 7 2
♢ A K Q 8 2	♢ A K Q 6 3 2	♢ A K Q 6 2
♣ 3	♣ 5	♣ Q J 5 2

One factor to take into account in a competitive auction at the three-level is the number of trumps held by your side. In general, it is worth bidding 3-over-their-3 when your side holds nine trumps. To make that judgement, one of the partners needs to know the combined trump length.

In former times, players would bid 2♠ over 2♡ on both hands (A) and (B). In that case if North pushes on to 3♡, East may be unsure of the combined spade length. With nine trumps a bid of 3♠ would be sensible, but with only eight trumps it is usually better to defend.

To solve this dilemma many pairs have adopted the 'support double' by opener: after a major suit response and a suit bid by next player below two of responder's major, double by opener promises 3-card support for responder's suit. Raising the suit guarantees 4-card support. Using support doubles:

(A) Bid 2♠. Shows a minimum opening with four spades.

(B) Double. Shows three spades exactly. Opener's strength is still wide-ranging. Might be a minimum opening, might be much stronger. The double is forcing and opener can reveal more later. For example, if responder bids 2♠, any further action by opener would show extras.

(C) Pass. Shows a minimum opening hand (you are too weak for 3♣) and implies fewer than three spades.

Tip 36: It is worth adding 'support doubles' to your system.

37   Dealer South : North-South vulnerable

WEST	NORTH	EAST	SOUTH
			No
1♣ (1)	No	1♡	1♠
No	2♠	Dble (2)	No
?			

(1) Playing a 15-17 1NT   (2) For takeout

What would you do as West with:

♠ K Q 10 6   ♡ A J 4   ◇ 10 9 6   ♣ Q 8 3

The deal comes from a qualifying round for a national final in 2003:

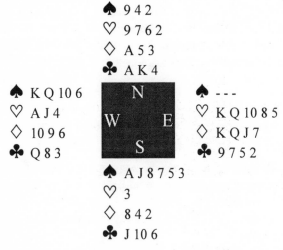

```
            ♠ 9 4 2
            ♡ 9 7 6 2
            ◇ A 5 3
            ♣ A K 4
♠ K Q 10 6              ♠ - - -
♡ A J 4                ♡ K Q 10 8 5
◇ 10 9 6               ◇ K Q J 7
♣ Q 8 3                ♣ 9 7 5 2
            ♠ A J 8 7 5 3
            ♡ 3
            ◇ 8 4 2
            ♣ J 10 6
```

West passed the double and led the ◇10, taken by the ace. A heart was led. East won, cashed two diamonds and reverted to hearts. South ruffed, played the ♣J – queen – king, ruffed another heart, cashed the ♣10 and crossed to the ♣A. With only ♠A-J-8-7 left, South played a spade to the ♠7 and ♠10. South had only one more loser and so made 2♠ doubled for a huge score.

Tip 37: Beware of playing for penalties below game-level when you hold 3+ support for partner's suit. (West might have made a support double over 1♠ – see Tip 36.)

38   Dealer South : North-South vulnerable

WEST	NORTH	EAST	SOUTH
			No
1♣	Dble	No	?

What should South do with:

♠ 6 4   ♡ J 5   ♢ J 8 4   ♣ 8 7 6 4 3 2

The fact that you have a tough problem does not mean that you can shirk your duty. With a hand in the 0-5 point range, reply to a takeout double with a suit bid. With no 4-card suit, bid your cheapest 3-card suit. Bid 1♢ here. The complete deal arose in a world championship:

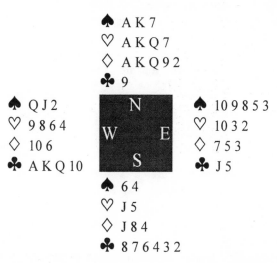

At one table South passed the double. North led a top spade and shifted to hearts. Declarer was allowed to ruff the fourth heart with the ♣J, escaping for two off. North-South collected +300, but this was a woeful result. At other tables, South responded 1♢, as recommended, and some Norths bid 6♢ there and then. No doubt South awaited the appearance of dummy with some trepidation, but 6♢ proved an easy make. Although South has only two jacks, what priceless gems they are.

Tip 38: Do not pass partner's takeout double with weak trumps.

39 Dealer South : North-South vulnerable

WEST	NORTH	EAST	SOUTH
			No
2♡ (1)	No	No	2♠
No	No	3♡	No
No	3♠	?	

(1) Weak-two, six hearts, 6-10 HCP

What would you do as East with:

♠ K 10 7   ♡ A 5 4   ◊ Q 8 4 2   ♣ 5 3 2

At pairs there is a tendency to make light penalty doubles at low levels, particularly if the opponents are vulnerable. If the opponents make it, it is only one board, about 4% of your total session score. As each board counts equally, an utter catastrophe and a bottom board is no worse than a modest error producing a bottom score. A bottom is a bottom – the size of the bottom is irrelevant. (Beware of puns in this area.)

The attraction is that if you defeat them by one trick when they are vulnerable, your +200 should be a top, outscoring all normal part-score results. If they are not vulnerable, you need to put them two down to obtain a top-notch score.

Nevertheless it does not pay to double a competent declarer at a low level if the high card strength is roughly equal unless you have a nasty surprise for declarer. A trump stack and a misfit with partner are the features for a successful low-level penalty. Otherwise you need a clear superiority in high card strength, say 23-17 or 24-16. Then the hand belongs to your side and if they outbid you, by all means double them to cater for the contract you might have made.

On borderline hands you will do well enough if you defeat their contract and achieve a plus score. If you can go plus on most of your marginal hands, your match-point score will be excellent without having to take any daredevil risks.

East should pass 3♠, but in fact doubled and the unsound double almost came off. Here is the full deal from the first officially recognized duplicate in the USSR in Leningrad in October, 1989:

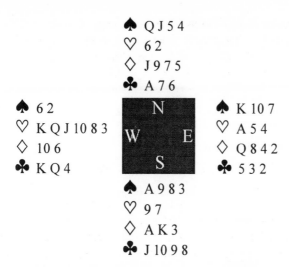

```
        ♠ Q J 5 4
        ♡ 6 2
        ◇ J 9 7 5
        ♣ A 7 6
♠ 6 2              ♠ K 10 7
♡ K Q J 10 8 3     ♡ A 5 4
◇ 10 6             ◇ Q 8 4 2
♣ K Q 4            ♣ 5 3 2
        ♠ A 9 8 3
        ♡ 9 7
        ◇ A K 3
        ♣ J 10 9 8
```

In the 'decadent West' South would open the bidding and West would
start with 1♡, not 2♡. When 2♡ is passed to South, the universal
expert choice would be a takeout double. East's double of 3♠ was,
no doubt, influenced by the vulnerability, but all the signs were
against a penalty double: too great a fit with partner, absence of a
trump stack and no preponderance of points. Even facing a 1♡
opening, a double of 3♠ would not be warranted.

West led the ♠6: jack – king – ace. A spade was returned to the
queen and a heart led. East rose with the ace and cashed the ♠10,
followed by a low heart, taken by West. The ♣K shift was won in
dummy and declarer came to hand with a diamond to continue with a
deceptive ♣9 (hoping West might duck and fall victim to an endplay
later). West took the ♣Q and exited with the third club.

South now knew that West had at most two diamonds and the points
revealed meant that East had the ◇Q. Declarer therefore ruffed his
last club in dummy and led the ◇J, pinning the ◇10. That old bridge
adage was proved right again: the pin is mightier than the axe.

**Tip 39: If the hand does not belong to your side, do not make a
penalty double at the 2-level or 3-level without a trump stack and
a misfit with partner's hand.**

40   Dealer North : North-South vulnerable

WEST	NORTH	EAST	SOUTH
	1♣ (1)	2♡ (2)	2NT (3)
?			

(1) Artificial, strong club
(2) Two-suiter, hearts and spades, weak
(3) Natural, forcing to game

What would you do as West with:

♠ 10   ♡ A 7 3 2   ◇ Q 10 6 5 3   ♣ A 8 7

This deal arose in the 2001 Bermuda Bowl match Italy vs USA:

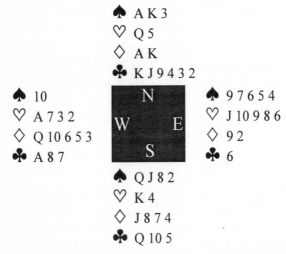

```
              ♠ A K 3
              ♡ Q 5
              ◇ A K
              ♣ K J 9 4 3 2

♠ 10             N          ♠ 9 7 6 5 4
♡ A 7 3 2     W     E       ♡ J 10 9 8 6
◇ Q 10 6 5 3     S          ◇ 9 2
♣ A 8 7                      ♣ 6

              ♠ Q J 8 2
              ♡ K 4
              ◇ J 8 7 4
              ♣ Q 10 5
```

East's courageous jump to 2♡ bore fruit when West correctly jumped to 4♡, passed by North and doubled by South. This contract was just one down for –100, with 5♣ unbeatable for North-South.

At the other table East timidly passed North's 1♣ opening and the bidding ended in 3NT by South. A heart lead would beat that, but West naturally led a diamond. 11 Imps to Italy, who won the match easily.

Tip 40: With a 9-card trump fit and one partner holding 10+ cards in two suits, jumping to game at once is also sound in competitive auctions (See Tip 24).

41   Dealer North : Both vulnerable

WEST	NORTH	EAST	SOUTH
No	1♣*	?	

*Artificial, strong club, 15+ points, any shape

What would you do as South with:

(A)	(B)	(C)
♠ Q J 9 6 4 2	♠ K J 9 3	♠ 7 5
♥ 7 4	♥ J 9 6 5 4 3	♥ A Q 9 7 2
♦ A Q 4 2	♦ 8 2	♦ J 6 5 4
♣ 3	♣ 9	♣ 9 5

Tip 40 illustrates the value of an aggressive interfering method over a strong 1♣. This is especially so if the opponents are using relays, which are very accurate for slam bidding. As game is unlikely your way, your primary aim is to destroy their methods or at least impede them. A good approach is to bid when weak (courage is a greater asset than points) and pass when strong (13+ points). Since the 1♣ opening is forcing, you will have a another chance to bid and your later action will confirm 13 points or more.

You want to be able to describe one-suiters and two-suiters and this structure works well:
All jumps in a suit are pre-emptive.
Non-jump bids show two-suiters, the suit bid and the next suit along:
1♦ = diamonds + hearts
1♥ = hearts + spades
1♠ = spades + clubs
2♣ = clubs + diamonds
The non-touching suits are shown by double (clubs + hearts) and 1NT (diamonds + spades). The minimum length in your suits should be 4-4, but a more shapely holding is recommended when vulnerable. If partner has passed and you have an almost worthless hand, you can take liberties. The opponents have at least game on and possibly slam.

On hearing the two-suiter, partner gives preference with three trumps or worse support. With 4-card support, raise to the two-level and with 5-card support, jump to the 3-level.

Using this approach you should bid 2♠ with (A). Even though this is a two-suiter, the spades are strong and the jump-bid takes up a lot of their space. With (B), bid 1♡, both majors, rather than 2♡, since the hearts are weak, and with (C), bid 1♢, showing the red suits.

In a major tournament in 2003, South passed with (B) and East-West had a free run to the unbeatable 6♣ for a great score.

WEST	EAST
♠ A 5 2	♠ 7
♡ 10 2	♡ A Q 8
♢ Q 7 6 5	♢ A K 10 3
♣ K J 10 3	♣ A Q 8 6 2

Had South bid 1♡, the bidding might have started:

W	N	E	S
	No	1♣	1♡
Dble	3♠ ...		

It would be much tougher for East-West to find a slam now.

In the same event, South did bid 1♢ with (C) on this deal:

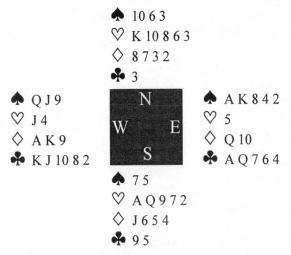

```
              ♠ 10 6 3
              ♡ K 10 8 6 3
              ♢ 8 7 3 2
              ♣ 3
  ♠ Q J 9          N          ♠ A K 8 4 2
  ♡ J 4                       ♡ 5
  ♢ A K 9     W       E       ♢ Q 10
  ♣ K J 10 8 2      S         ♣ A Q 7 6 4
              ♠ 7 5
              ♡ A Q 9 7 2
              ♢ J 6 5 4
              ♣ 9 5
```

After 1♣ : 1♢, West showed a strong hand with no short suit and North jumped to 3♡. This was passed back to West who doubled. East-West collected +500, not nearly as good as 6♣ or 6♠ their way.

Tip 41: Have a good obstructive system available against strong 1♣ openings and use the system aggressively.

42   Dealer West : Nil vulnerable

WEST	NORTH	EAST	SOUTH
1♡	2NT*	?	

*Weak, at least 5-5 in the minors

What would you do as East with:

♠ K 8 2   ♡ K 9 7 5 3   ◇ 9   ♣ A 7 4 2

Showing a two-suiter with the Unusual 2NT is part and parcel of the duplicate world and you need to be able to cope effectively with this interference. There are many possible schemes. This one works well:

Double = Aiming for penalties. All later doubles are for penalties. Responder is strong in at least one of the minors. If South bids a minor, West is expected to double if strong in that minor, otherwise pass and give East a chance to double. Responder will not have support for opener's suit.

3♣ = At least game-inviting with hearts
3◇ = At least game-inviting with spades
3♡ = Hearts, but weaker than the 3♣ response
3♠ = Spades, but weaker than the 3◇ response
3NT / 4♡ / 4♠ = To play
4♣ / 4◇ = Splinter, a strong raise of opener's major, 4+ trumps and a singleton or void in the suit bid

Pass followed by double of 3♣ or 3◇ later is for takeout. If you are looking for penalties, double 2NT first.

Using these methods, East would splinter with 4◇. The layout:

WEST	EAST	W	N	E	S
♠ A 5 3	♠ K 8 2	1♡	2NT	4◇	Dble
♡ A Q 8 6 2	♡ K 9 7 5 3	4NT	No	5♡*	No
◇ 8 6 5 3	◇ 9	6♡	No	No	No
♣ K	♣ A 7 4 2	*2 key cards, no trump queen			

Tip 42: Make sure that you and partner have a comprehensive defence to the Unusual 2NT overcall.

43   Dealer West : Both vulnerable

WEST	NORTH	EAST	SOUTH
1♠	2♠*	?	

*Michaels Cue-Bid, 5+ hearts and a 5+ minor

What would you do as East with:

♠ A Q 6 4   ♡ K 8 5   ◇ K 9 8 6   ♣ J 2

The Michaels Cue-Bid is very popular, particularly over a major opening. 1♠ : (2♠) or 1♡ : (2♡) shows 5+ cards in the other major and at least five cards in one of the minors. Do you have a system in place to deal with such intervention? Here, too, several methods exist. Here is one of the better ones:

Double = Looking for penalties. You can play 1♠ : (2♠) : Double as equivalent to 1♠ : (Double) : Redouble. Responder should be short in opener's suit, with about 10+ HCP and the ability to double at least one of their suits for penalties.

3-of-opener's-major = Weak, pre-emptive (about 0-5/6 points)
4-of-opener's-major = Weak, pre-emptive, like 1-major : 4-major
2NT = Good raise of opener's major with about 6/7-9 points
Their-major at cheapest level = Stronger raise, 10+ HCP
Jump-their-major or 4♣ / 4◇ = Splinter raise
3♣ or 3◇ = Natural, forcing
3NT = To play
Pass and double later is for takeout. If you want to look for penalties, double at once.

Using these methods, East would show a good raise with 3♡.

WEST	EAST	W	N	E	S
♠ K J 9 7 2	♠ A Q 6 4	1♠	2♠	3♡	No
♡ A 6 4	♡ K 8 5	3♠	No	4♠*	All pass
◇ A J	◇ K 9 8 6				
♣ 9 8 3	♣ J 2				

*Take away either red king and East would pass 3♠.

Tip 43: Make sure that you and partner have agreed on sound countermeasures against the Michaels Cue-Bid.

44   Dealer South : East-West vulnerable

WEST	NORTH	EAST	SOUTH
			No
No	2♡*	?	

*Weak two-opening

What would you do as East with:

♠ K ♡ A 7 ◇ 8 5 4 3 2 ♣ K 10 9 7 2

It is very tempting to compete after a weak opening, especially after a pass on your left and a pre-empt on your right, as partner is marked with some strength. That is precisely the drawback to taking action with sub-minimum values. What you bid may well work, but partner will almost always tend to bid and push you too high. See what happened on this deal from the final of the 2002 Women's World Pairs:

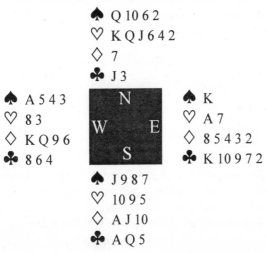

East should have passed 2♡ but could not resist a 3♣ overcall. South bid 3♡ and West doubled, showing values but primarily for takeout. East bid 4◇ and South doubled for penalties. East was two down, −500, for an absolute bottom. Had East passed, N-S would probably play a heart part-score for +170 and a 60% score to E-W.

Tip 44: Beware weak action when partner is marked with strength.

45   Dealer South : Nil vulnerable

WEST	NORTH	EAST	SOUTH
			1NT (1)
2◇ (2)	?		

(1) 15-17
(2) Shows both majors

What should North do with:

♠ 8 7   ♡ 5   ◇ A K Q 8 7 4   ♣ Q 8 4 2

You will encounter interference more and more after a 1NT opening. You need a good structure to make the most of your assets and to compete effectively. Most top pairs use 2NT artificially, either to show a weak competing or a good hand indicating whether a stopper is held in the enemy suit. This powerful method (Rubensohl) allows you to use transfers at the three-level, including 2NT as a transfer to clubs:

2NT = 5+ clubs, may be competitive, may be strong
3♣   = transfer to diamonds
3◇   = transfer to hearts
3♡   = transfer to spades
3♠   = artificial, no stopper and no 4-card major
3NT = natural, no 4-card major but a stopper in their suit(s)
Exception: Bidding the suit below their suit replaces Stayman and shows at least one 4-card major.

After opener accepts a transfer, responder can bid a second suit, bid 3NT to show a stopper in their suit or bid the enemy suit to deny a stopper there. With the hand above, responder bids 3♣, transfer to diamonds, and over 3◇, bids 3♡ to ask for a stopper there. Opener can then bid 3NT (stoppers in both majors), 3♠ (hearts stopped, but asking for a stopper in spades) or 4♣ / 4◇ natural, denying a stopper in hearts.

As 2NT has been lost, you can double to show game-inviting values. Suit bids at the two-level are merely competitive. If their intervention is 2♣, use 'double' to say, 'I would have bid 2♣' and all other bids retain their system meaning. Thus you can play your normal system after a 2♣ overcall, whether 2♣ is natural or artificial.

Tip 45: Rubensohl is highly effective when they bid over your 1NT.

46   Dealer South : East-West vulnerable

WEST	NORTH	EAST	SOUTH
			No
2♣ (1)	Dble (2)	No	?

(1) 10-14 points, 6+ clubs, no second suit
(2) For takeout

What would you do as South with:

♠ 9 7 6 5   ♡ - - -   ◇ A Q 10 9 5   ♣ Q 9 8 6

Because of the good shape South is worth a jump to 4♠, but the danger is that North might hold only three spades. The better action is to bid 3♣ to show a hand playable in more than one suit. When South later removes 4♡ to 4♠, the message should be clear that South is giving North a choice between spades and diamonds.

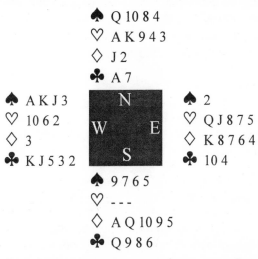

                    ♠ Q 10 8 4
                    ♡ A K 9 4 3
                    ◇ J 2
                    ♣ A 7

♠ A K J 3   ♠ 2
♡ 10 6 2   ♡ Q J 8 7 5
◇ 3   ◇ K 8 7 6 4
♣ K J 5 3 2   ♣ 10 4

                    ♠ 9 7 6 5
                    ♡ - - -
                    ◇ A Q 10 9 5
                    ♣ Q 9 8 6

In a national selection event in 2003 South bid 3♣, North jumped to 4♡, South removed to 4♠ and West doubled, all pass. A few slips later, South had ten tricks. West led ◇3: jack – king (not good) – ace. South played ♠5 – 3 – 4 – 2 (South should overtake with ♠8 to play ♡A, ♡K, heart ruff). Then came ◇9, ruffed, followed by a low club (not good at all). West should play ♣A, ♠K and exit with a heart.

Tip 46: Bid their suit to show a hand with more than one option.

Dealer East : Both vulnerable

WEST	NORTH	EAST	SOUTH
		3♣	?

What would you do as South with:

(A)   (B)   (C)

♠ Q J 8 4 2   ♠ 4   ♠ Q J 8 4 2
♡ A 3   ♡ Q J 8 4 2   ♡ A K J 7 5
◇ A K J 7 5   ◇ A K J 7 5   ◇ A 3
♣ 4   ♣ A 3   ♣ 4

Most pairs use double for takeout after a three-level opening. The hand type is normally one which is short in their suit and has support for the missing suits. Ideally the pattern is 4-4-4-1 or 5-4-4-0, but one has to make do with a 4-4-3-2 or 5-4-3-1 if the strength is right. For action at the three-level, a 6-loser hand or better is appropriate. Conventional wisdom is to play partner for two tricks after an enemy pre-emptive opening. If partner does have the two tricks expected, that will bring your loser tally down from six to four and that should give you nine tricks.

The takeout double is usually not suitable for very shapely hands such as 5-5 or 6-5. The danger of the double is that partner bids too much in the unbid suit in which you are short. To cope with such hands, some players bid just one suit and hope to have a chance to show the other suit later. That is not particularly attractive on any of the above hands, since the Q-J-8-4-2 suit is not very strong.

One way to deal with this is to bid the enemy suit. Many pairs would use a bid of 4♣ here to show a two-suiter with both majors. Bidding their suit can cover more problem hands if you extend it to cover any pronounced two-suiter. Thus you would bid 4♣ on each of the hands above. If partner bids 4♡ opposite (A), you bid 4♠, showing spades and diamonds. If you hear 4♠ opposite (B), bid 5◇ to show hearts and diamonds. Likewise with (C), after 4◇, remove to 4♡.

Tip 47: After an opposing three-level pre-empt it is sensible to use a bid of their suit to show a two-suiter, at least a 5-5 pattern.

48   Dealer East : North-South vulnerable

WEST	NORTH	EAST	SOUTH
		4♠	?

What would you do as South with:

(A)	(B)	(C)
♠ A 7 6	♠ 2	♠ - - -
♡ A K 10 4	♡ A J 10 4	♡ A K J 7 3
◇ 7 2	◇ A Q 9 8 6	◇ A Q J 6 4 3
♣ K Q 6 4	♣ A K 2	♣ 5 4

Every partnership will have agreed on the meaning of a double after a four-level pre-empt. Some use it for penalties, others to show any strong hand, but the dominant approach among top players is to use double for takeout even at this level. The theory is that you are much more likely to pick up a hand short in the pre-empt suit than one that has length and/or strength in that suit. Since the aim of bidding methods at duplicate is to cover the most frequent situations, double for takeout has it all over doubling for penalties.

A takeout double of a 4♣ or 4◇ opening should be at least 4-4 in the majors. If you are doubling 4♡ for takeout, partner will expect you to have four spades. If you are doubling 4♠, you might have just three cards in one of the unbid suits, since partner should not be inclined to reply at the 5-level without a 5+ suit.

If you and partner have agreed to play double for takeout, then:

(A) Pass. You are strong enough to take action, but you have too many spades and not enough diamonds for a takeout double. You might survive a double – you would be very happy if partner left the double in – but the risk is significant. Playing double for takeout does mean that you might miss penalties occasionally.

(B) Double. Typical values for this level of takeout double. You will not be dismayed if partner passes the double for penalties.

(C) 4NT. This is used here to show an extreme two-suiter, at least 5-5.

Tip 48: Play double for takeout after their four-level pre-empt.

49   Dealer West : North-South vulnerable

WEST	NORTH	EAST	SOUTH
1♠	No	4♠	Dble*
No	?		

*For takeout

What would you do as North with:

(A)
♠ J 10 7 6
♡ 10 4
♢ Q J 7 2
♣ Q 6 4

(B)
♠ 8 5 4
♡ J 10 4
♢ 9 6 5
♣ Q 6 5 2

(C)
♠ 7 3 2
♡ A 7
♢ K 8 7 2
♣ Q 7 5 3

Since the jump-raise to game is a pre-emptive move, most pairs will play the double by fourth hand the same as though there had been a four-level pre-emptive opening. South's double then should be the same hand type that would make a takeout double of a 4♠ opening.

If partner has doubled 4♡ for takeout, you would be keen to bid 4♠ with 4+ spades, but less eager to push to 5♣ or 5♢. Similarly, when partner is doubling 4♠ for takeout, you are generally reluctant to bid to the five-level unless you have something worth bidding. Imagine partner has a 4-4-4-1 pattern, short in their suit, and about five losers. If you can then visualize a good trump fit your way or a double fit, by all means go ahead and bid. With no double fit likely, bid only with a 5+ suit. Otherwise pass and defend. With partner's expected strength, their contract is likely to fail most of the time. On that basis:

(A) Pass. You have no long suit, your hand is balanced and you have a likely trick in their suit. Playing for penalties is probably best.

(B) Pass. The hand is too flat and too weak to push to the five-level.

(C) Bid 4NT. In reply to a takeout double at the four-level, 4NT is used to show a hand which has more than one playable suit. This should ensure you reach the better minor suit contract.

Tip 49: After a takeout double at the four-level note the use of 4NT to offer a choice of contracts.

50   Dealer West : North-South vulnerable

WEST	NORTH	EAST	SOUTH
1♠	No	4♠	Dble*
No	5♦	No	?

*For takeout

What would you do as South with:

♠ - - -   ♡ A K 4   ♦ A 10 3 2   ♣ A K J 7 5 4

A sensible agreement is to play doubles for takeout if they bid and raise a suit directly and after any pre-emptive bid. Here 4♠ is a direct raise and pre-emptive as well, and so doubling for takeout is popular among top players. In reply partner will tend to pass for penalties with a balanced hand or with strength in their suit. If partner takes out the double to the five-level, you can expect partner to hold a 5+ suit.

When deciding whether to leave it at the five-level or push on to slam, consider how much better your hand is than it might have been for the initial double. As double can be expected to be a strong 4-4-4-1, you have three features here better than a minimum double: you have a void in their suit, not a singleton; you have first-round control in every suit; you have a source of tricks in another suit, the clubs, which partner should be able to set up to discard losers elsewhere. You have more than enough to raise to 6♦. The two hands:

Partner	You
♠ Q 3	♠ - - -
♡ 9 7 2	♡ A K 4
♦ K 9 8 6 5 4	♦ A 10 3 2
♣ 8 3	♣ A K J 7 5 4

Partner has done well to bid 5♦ and 6♦ should be easy. If trumps are 2-1, you are almost certain to make thirteen tricks. It is very hard to find a good grand slam after this much pre-emption, but the small slam should be reached. Note how much more effective your takeout double is (Tip 48) than a bid of 5♣, which partner would pass.

Tip 50: When deciding whether to bid on after a reply to your double, consider how much better your hand is than it might be.

51   Dealer East : North-South vulnerable

WEST	NORTH	EAST	SOUTH
		1♡	2♠*
4♡	4♠	5♡	No
No	5♠	6♡	No
No	?		

*Weak jump-overcall

What would you do as North with:

♠ 9 7 6 4 3   ♡ - - -   ◇ A Q J 5 3   ♣ 6 5 2

Opposite a weak jump-overcall, even though it will be respectable at this vulnerability, you cannot reasonably expect to make 6♠. On the other hand you have very little defence against 6♡. In a national selection event in 2003, one North bid 6♠. This was the deal:

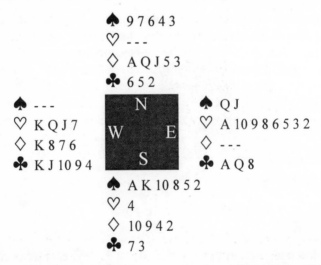

```
            ♠ 9 7 6 4 3
            ♡ - - -
            ◇ A Q J 5 3
            ♣ 6 5 2
♠ - - -           N         ♠ Q J
♡ K Q J 7                   ♡ A 10 9 8 6 5 3 2
◇ K 8 7 6    W       E      ◇ - - -
♣ K J 10 9 4      S         ♣ A Q 8
            ♠ A K 10 8 5 2
            ♡ 4
            ◇ 10 9 4 2
            ♣ 7 3
```

East doubled, but West unwisely led a heart. Declarer ruffed, drew trumps and repeated diamond finesses allowed 6♠ to make. West's bidding and lead were both less than ideal. At other tables East-West played in 6♡. One West splintered with 4♠ over 2♠ and that led to 7♡ making. Note the power of the voids for each side.

Tip 51: With a key void, be prepared to bid one more.

52   Dealer West : East-West vulnerable

WEST	NORTH	EAST	SOUTH
1♠	2♡	2♠	3♡
3♠	4♡	No	No
4♠	?		

What would you do as North with:

♠ - - -   ♡ A Q J 9 7 4 3   ◇ K 8 4   ♣ 7 6 2

Because of the void in spades it seems that there is a sensational fit your way and, following Tip 51, you should bid 5♡. This ignores the fact that you have a partner and you do not know how strong partner is in spades. In practice, North bid 5♡, passed to West, who doubled.

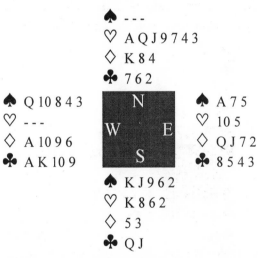

         ♠ - - -
         ♡ A Q J 9 7 4 3
         ◇ K 8 4
         ♣ 7 6 2

♠ Q 10 8 4 3   ♠ A 7 5
♡ - - -   ♡ 10 5
◇ A 10 9 6   ◇ Q J 7 2
♣ A K 10 9   ♣ 8 5 4 3

         ♠ K J 9 6 2
         ♡ K 8 6 2
         ◇ 5 3
         ♣ Q J

5♡ was only one off, but that was little comfort as 4♠ is in deep trouble on repeated heart leads and should be at least two down. Had East bid 4♠ and South passed it to North, it would be sensible to bid 5♡, but in the direct seat North should pass the decision to partner.

Tip 52: When faced with a decision whether or not to compete higher, the player short in the enemy suit should not take action in the direct seat but should leave the decision to partner, who holds length in the enemy suit.

53   Dealer North : North-South vulnerable

WEST	NORTH	EAST	SOUTH
	1◇	No	1♡
3♠	4♡	4♠	No
No	?		

What action would you take as North with:

♠ 4 2   ♡ A K 10 4   ◇ A K 10 9 4   ♣ A 10

West's 3♠ pre-empt has truncated your bidding space and you are much stronger for your 4♡ bid than you might have been. There is a good chance that partner has a singleton spade and if so, you might well be able to make 5♡. It is almost certain that a score of +650 will be more than what you might obtain from doubling 4♠. Despite any misgivings, however, the right action is to double. The deal arose in a strong selection tournament in 2003:

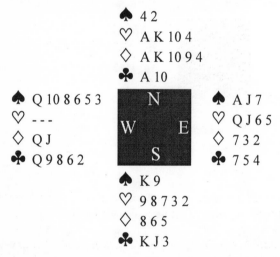

                    ♠ 4 2
                    ♡ A K 10 4
                    ◇ A K 10 9 4
                    ♣ A 10

♠ Q 10 8 6 5 3   ♠ A J 7
♡ - - -   ♡ Q J 6 5
◇ Q J   ◇ 7 3 2
♣ Q 9 8 6 2   ♣ 7 5 4

                    ♠ K 9
                    ♡ 9 8 7 3 2
                    ◇ 8 6 5
                    ♣ K J 3

Quite a number went on to 5♡, which fails by one trick. Doubling 4♠ will bring in 300 or 500. It is true that the heart layout is unlucky, but then the diamond position is very lucky. In addition, South might have had only four hearts.

Tip 53: Do not push to the 5-level with a doubleton in their suit.

54   Dealer West : East-West vulnerable

WEST	NORTH	EAST	SOUTH
No	No	4♡	4NT*
5♡	?		

*For takeout, shows both minors, at least 5-5

What would you do as North with:

♠ A 10 9 3 2   ♡ - - -   ◇ A 9 7 2   ♣ 9 6 5 4

It seems as though the opponents have over-reached themselves. You are looking at two aces and partner has to have some values for that 4NT bid. In a national event in 2003, North was seduced into doubling 5♡.

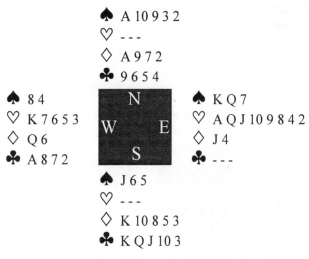

It is true that 5♡ can be defeated, but not when South makes the normal lead of the ♣K. At this vulnerability it pays to trust the opponents.

To avoid this calamity North should bid 5NT, asking South to pick the preferred minor. South will bid 6♣, which West will double. The defence can take 6♣ two down, but South might escape for one off. Either result is an improvement on –850.

Tip 54: It is wise to trust the opponents who bid to a high level at unfavourable vulnerability. Beware of speculative doubles here.

55   Dealer East : North-South vulnerable

WEST	NORTH	EAST	SOUTH
		1♠	2♡
2♣	4♡	4♠	?

What would you do as South with:

♠ --- ♡ A J 10 8 7 5 ◊ A Q J 9 8 ♣ 10 3

You have a good case for trying for a slam. Firstly, you might make
it. If you need a red-suit finesse, it is likely to work on the bidding.
Secondly, they may sacrifice in 6♠ at the vulnerability. As you have
first-round control in three suits, you could jump straight to 6♡, but
that is not the best move.

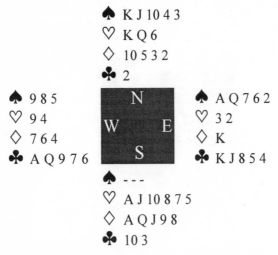

```
                    ♠ K J 10 4 3
                    ♡ K Q 6
                    ◊ 10 5 3 2
                    ♣ 2
    ♠ 9 8 5            N            ♠ A Q 7 6 2
    ♡ 9 4         W       E         ♡ 3 2
    ◊ 7 6 4                         ◊ K
    ♣ A Q 9 7 6        S            ♣ K J 8 5 4
                    ♠ - - -
                    ♡ A J 10 8 7 5
                    ◊ A Q J 9 8
                    ♣ 10 3
```

To jump to 6♡ effectively telegraphs your void to the opponents. If
you intend to bid six anyway, you might as well bid 4NT first and bid
six after the reply. That may give you a favourable lead. If you jump
to 6♡ here, West might lead the ♣A. If you use 4NT, West may feel
no rush to lead an ace and start with a spade. Now with trumps 2-2
and the ◊K with East, as expected, you can make all thirteen tricks.

**Tip 55: If you have a void and are worth a small slam only, using
4NT for aces or key cards first may produce a favourable lead.**

56   Dealer East : Both vulnerable

WEST   NORTH   EAST   SOUTH
                      1♠   ?

What would you do as South with:

(A)   (B)   (C)
♠ 3   ♠ K 9 4 2   ♠ K J 4
♡ K J 10 4 3   ♡ K J 10 4 3   ♡ A K 7 6 2
◇ K 9 4 2   ◇ Q J 5   ◇ 8 6 3
♣ 8 4 3   ♣ 9   ♣ 5 4

A two-level overcall is expected to have 10+ points and a strong suit. The high card points can be reduced slightly for a strong 6+ suit. Feel free to overcall on light values when you are short in opener's suit. The risk of a penalty is negligible, as third hand figures to have support for opener. On that basis a 2♡ overcall is reasonable with (A), but pass with (B) and (C) because of the length and strength in spades.

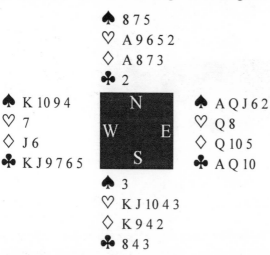

```
              ♠ 8 7 5
              ♡ A 9 6 5 2
              ◇ A 8 7 3
              ♣ 2
♠ K 10 9 4         N          ♠ A Q J 6 2
♡ 7                           ♡ Q 8
◇ J 6       W          E      ◇ Q 10 5
♣ K J 9 7 6 5      S          ♣ A Q 10
              ♠ 3
              ♡ K J 10 4 3
              ◇ K 9 4 2
              ♣ 8 4 3
```

After (1♠) : 2♡, West might bid 4♠ and North 5♡. This is one down with 4♠ unbeatable. If East-West bid on to 5♠, that can be defeated. If South passes and it goes (1♠) : No : (4♠), will North bid?

Tip 56: Overcall freely with modest values if short in their suit(s).

81

57   Dealer North : East-West vulnerable

WEST	NORTH	EAST	SOUTH
	No	1♡	Dble
?			

Your agreed methods include 3♡ as a pre-emptive raise and 2NT as a limit raise or stronger. What action would you take as West with:

♠ 9 8   ♡ K 9 7 5   ◇ 5 3 2   ♣ K J 10 4

In expert circles the jump-raise is popular nowadays as a pre-emptive raise even if there is no intervening double. The expectancy for this pre-empt is 0-5 high card points and 4+ trumps. West is too weak for 2NT and too strong for 3♡. The best move is 2♡, showing 6-9 points. On this deal from the 1998 world championships West made a pre-emptive jump to 3♡ with calamitous consequences:

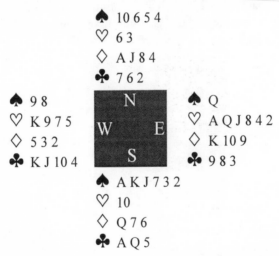

West led the ♡K (a low heart might be better) and East overtook with the ♡A. Judging West could not have so much in clubs and make a pre-emptive raise, East played a futile second heart. South ruffed and was able to discard a club later on the thirteenth diamond. A switch at trick 2 to a top club would have defeated the contract.

Tip 57: Do not mislead partner as to your strength, lest partner errs.

58   Dealer North : Both vulnerable

WEST	NORTH	EAST	SOUTH
	No	No	4♡
?			

If your methods here include double for takeout, what would you do as West with these cards:

♠ A J 10 4   ♡ Q J 6   ◇ 9 8   ♣ A Q 10 3

Although double is for takeout, there is natural temptation to double with a strong hand to try to score good penalties. There is nothing wrong with this temptation as long as you do not give in. In the final of 2002 Women's World Pairs West did succumb and was punished:

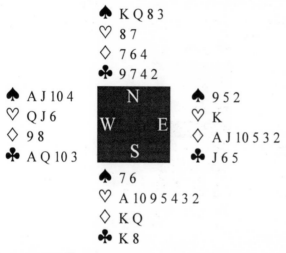

```
              ♠ K Q 8 3
              ♡ 8 7
              ◇ 7 6 4
              ♣ 9 7 4 2
  ♠ A J 10 4        N        ♠ 9 5 2
  ♡ Q J 6      W         E   ♡ K
  ◇ 9 8                      ◇ A J 10 5 3 2
  ♣ A Q 10 3        S        ♣ J 6 5
              ♠ 7 6
              ♡ A 10 9 5 4 3 2
              ◇ K Q
              ♣ K 8
```

West doubled 4♡ (for takeout) and East naturally removed to 5◇, which was passed out. After ♡A and another heart, declarer finessed in diamonds. South shifted to a spade, taken by the ace and when the next diamond finesse lost, declarer was –200. That was worth 4 match-points out of 30, about 13%. Had West found a disciplined pass of 4♡, she would have collected +200 and 21/30 match-points, 70%.

Tip 58: If you play doubles of high-level pre-empts for takeout, then be prepared to pass and defend with a strong, balanced hand.

59   Dealer North : East-West vulnerable

WEST	NORTH	EAST	SOUTH
	No	No	1♣
Dble	?		

What would you do as South with:

♠ K 7 2   ♡ - - -   ◊ A 9 7 6   ♣ 10 9 5 4 3 2

There are two guides which should lead you into jumping straight to game. With ten trumps and a weak hand, bidding to game at once works well, either as a sacrifice or if it happens to make. Therefore bid 5♣. The deal arose in a national championship in 2002:

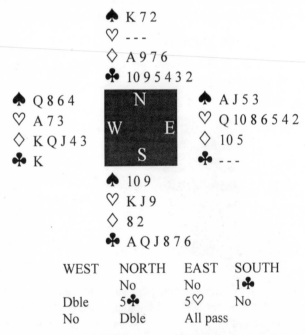

	♠ K 7 2		
	♡ - - -		
	◊ A 9 7 6		
	♣ 10 9 5 4 3 2		

♠ Q 8 6 4   ♠ A J 5 3
♡ A 7 3   ♡ Q 10 8 6 5 4 2
◊ K Q J 4 3   ◊ 10 5
♣ K   ♣ - - -

♠ 10 9
♡ K J 9
◊ 8 2
♣ A Q J 8 7 6

WEST	NORTH	EAST	SOUTH
	No	No	1♣
Dble	5♣	5♡	No
No	Dble	All pass	

You can hardly blame East for bidding 5♡, but declarer had to lose two hearts and a diamond, +200 and a great score to North-South.

You do not need to wait for an opposition bid before jumping to game when you know you have ten combined trumps. With a weak hand, the sooner you do it the better.

84

Dealer North   ♠ K J 2
Both vulnerable   ♥ 10 7
                     ♦ K Q 9 5 4 2
                     ♣ 9 7

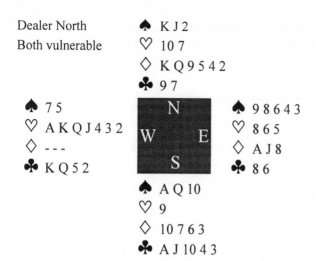

West	East
♠ 7 5	♠ 9 8 6 4 3
♥ A K Q J 4 3 2	♥ 8 6 5
♦ - - -	♦ A J 8
♣ K Q 5 2	♣ 8 6

                     ♠ A Q 10
                     ♥ 9
                     ♦ 10 7 6 3
                     ♣ A J 10 4 3

In the same event North opened 2♦, weak, and South jumped to 5♦.
West bid 5♥ (wouldn't you?). South doubled and collected +200.

Dealer North   ♠ A Q J 5 3
E-W vulnerable   ♥ Q 10 8
                     ♦ J
                     ♣ K 7 6 4

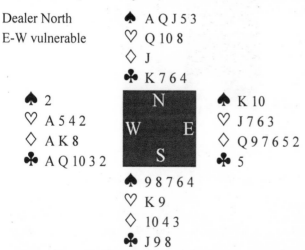

West	East
♠ 2	♠ K 10
♥ A 5 4 2	♥ J 7 6 3
♦ A K 8	♦ Q 9 7 6 5 2
♣ A Q 10 3 2	♣ 5

                     ♠ 9 8 7 6 4
                     ♥ K 9
                     ♦ 10 4 3
                     ♣ J 9 8

In the final of the 2002 World Women's Pairs, North opened 1♠ and
some Souths bid 2♠ or 3♠. Best is to bite the bullet and jump to 4♠
at once for maximum pressure. Note that 4♥ East-West is unbeatable.

Tip 59: With ten trumps and a weak hand, jump to game at once.

60   Dealer South : Both vulnerable

WEST	NORTH	EAST	SOUTH
			2♦ (1)
No	4♥ (2)	No	No
?			

(1) Multi-2♦, weak two in hearts or spades
(2) Pass with hearts, bid 4♠ with spades

What action would you take as West with these cards:

♠ A 6 4 3   ♥ 2   ♦ Q 8 6   ♣ A Q 8 6 4

West is not strong enough to come in at once over the 2♦ opening, but the situation has changed. It seems that North-South have found a good trump fit. In that case your side should have good fit, too.

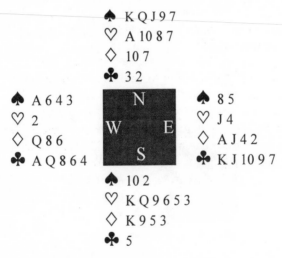

North bid game, as North-South were sure to have a 10+ fit. In practice, West passed, with 4♥ unbeatable. West should double for takeout. There is risk attached, of course, but these are the risks you must take regularly in the competitive battle. East will bid 5♣, or 4NT (showing two playable suits – see Tip 49) and West will bid 5♣, a good sacrifice.

Tip 60: If the bidding reveals that they probably have a strong trump fit, compete fiercely when you are short in their suit.

Part 3: OPENING LEADS

In no other area of the play of the cards is there such a marked difference in strategy between the pairs game and either teams or rubber bridge as with the opening lead. At teams or rubber bridge, your objectives are clearcut: declarer's task is to make the contract and overtricks are a minor consideration; the task of the defence is to defeat the contract – conceding an overtrick to try to achieve that objective is an acceptable loss.

The approach to the defence at pairs is radically different. It may be some time before we can tell what is our objective. Is it to defeat the contract *OR* to hold declarer to the contract *OR* to give away no more than a specific number of overtricks? We can rarely tell which of these is our objective when it comes to choosing the opening lead. Our only clues lie in the bidding.

One thing is sure: we cannot afford to be generous, light-hearted or carefree with the opening lead. To give away a precious overtrick with our lead is an opportunity squandered. That might be the difference between a good score and a below-average result. Recovery from a bad start may be impossible. The best match-point players are very, very frugal with their opening leads.

61   Dealer East : East-West vulnerable

WEST	NORTH	EAST	SOUTH
		No	1♡
No	2♡	No	3♣*
No	3♡	All pass	

*Long-suit trial

What would you lead as West from:

♠ A 8 3   ♡ Q 9 2   ◇ A 9 3 2   ♣ Q 10 2

With no attractive lead, you usually choose the least of evils, giving due consideration to the auction. A long-suit trial bid is normally made in a 3-card or 4-card suit where opener needs help. Usually opener will have two or three losers in that suit. Make up your mind what to lead before looking at the complete deal:

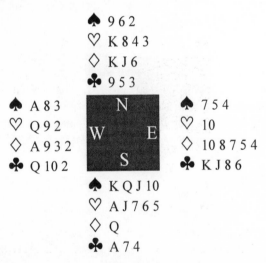

At the table West chose the ◇A. That was fatal, as declarer could now discard two club losers on dummy's diamond winners and make an overtrick. The ♠A lead would also allow the contract to succeed. Only a club gives the defence enough tricks in time.

Tip 61: If declarer has made a long-suit trial bid, which has been rejected by dummy, leading the trial suit often works well.

62 The opposition bidding goes like this:

SOUTH	NORTH		
2◇ (1)	2NT (2)	(1) 2◇	= game-force, 23+ points
3♣ (3)	3◇ (4)	(2) 2NT	= natural, positive reply
3♠	3NT	(3) 3♣	= Stayman
6♠	No	(4) 3◇	= No 4-card major

What would you lead as West from:

♠ 8   ♡ 9 7 4   ◇ A 8 6 4 3 2   ♣ Q 10 8

This deal comes from a pairs event and any of twelve cards would have defeated the slam. Declarer scored a top when West unwisely chose the ◇A lead.

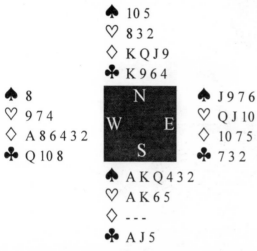

```
                    ♠ 10 5
                    ♡ 8 3 2
                    ◇ K Q J 9
                    ♣ K 9 6 4
      ♠ 8                         ♠ J 9 7 6
      ♡ 9 7 4          N          ♡ Q J 10
      ◇ A 8 6 4 3 2  W   E        ◇ 10 7 5
      ♣ Q 10 8          S         ♣ 7 3 2
                    ♠ A K Q 4 3 2
                    ♡ A K 6 5
                    ◇ - - -
                    ♣ A J 5
```

Even a club lead into declarer's tenace would not be fatal. South's failure to use Blackwood was a clue that South might have a void. (Corollary: It may pay to use Blackwood even with a void if you intend bidding the slam regardless – see Tip 55.)

Tip 62: At pairs, ace leads against a small slam are more attractive than usual. Still, beware of leading an ace against 6NT (the ace will usually not run away) or leading an ace if an opponent has jumped to slam without asking for aces / key cards.

63 The opposition have bid 2♣ : 3♢, 3NT. Your lead from:

♠ J 10 9 6 5 4 2   ♡ Q 6   ♢ 8 4 3   ♣ 6

Playing teams you might start with the ♡Q, the best chance to defeat 3NT. On some lucky day you will find partner with A-J-10-x-x over dummy's K-x-x, or with ♡K-J-x-x-x and a miraculous entry. Playing pairs you should lead the humdrum ♠J. There is no hope that a spade lead can beat 3NT. Partner can hardly have three spades and even if you set the spades up, you have no entry to cash them. As the opposition bidding reveals almost enough for a slam, there is virtually no realistic hope of beating 3NT and so you should make the safe spade lead.

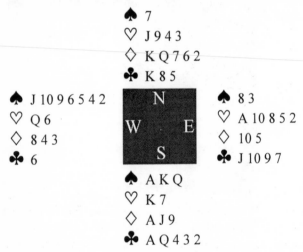

```
              ♠ 7
              ♡ J 9 4 3
              ♢ K Q 7 6 2
              ♣ K 8 5
♠ J 10 9 6 5 4 2          ♠ 8 3
♡ Q 6         N           ♡ A 10 8 5 2
♢ 8 4 3    W     E        ♢ 10 5
♣ 6           S           ♣ J 10 9 7
              ♠ A K Q
              ♡ K 7
              ♢ A J 9
              ♣ A Q 4 3 2
```

South has eleven tricks on top. A heart lead gives South twelve tricks. Even worse, if East unwisely ducks the ♡Q, South can squeeze East and make thirteen tricks. It is true that declarer can make twelve tricks also on a spade lead, but in real life no declarer is going to lead a heart to the king and risk making only eleven or even ten tricks. On the spade lead South is likely to run the diamonds and pitch the hearts, hoping for all the tricks. All East must do is hold on to the four clubs and the ♡A.

Tip 63 (a): If you have a choice between a safe lead, highly unlikely to beat the contract, and a speculative lead which might do so, stick with the safe lead. The speculative lead may cost an overtrick.

South opens 1NT in third seat and all pass. You to lead from:

♠ Q 9 8   ♡ Q 9 8   ◇ 8 7 5   ♣ K Q 9 5

You have no outstanding choice. In such a case it is usually best to lead the suit that is least revolting. Here that would be a diamond. This does not aim to develop any tricks for your side, but it is least likely to give away a trick. The complete deal:

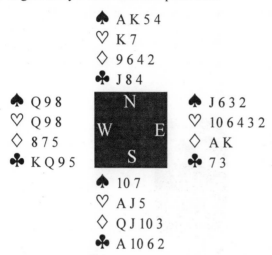

```
                ♠ A K 5 4
                ♡ K 7
                ◇ 9 6 4 2
                ♣ J 8 4
  ♠ Q 9 8                        ♠ J 6 3 2
  ♡ Q 9 8          N             ♡ 10 6 4 3 2
  ◇ 8 7 5       W     E          ◇ A K
  ♣ K Q 9 5        S             ♣ 7 3
                ♠ 10 7
                ♡ A J 5
                ◇ Q J 10 3
                ♣ A 10 6 2
```

In a pairs tournament half the field led a club and at those tables declarer generally made nine tricks, especially on the ♣K lead when declarer won and finessed the ♣8 next to score three club tricks. The rest led a diamond, won by East who switched, usually to hearts. The play then became a tussle for the eighth trick. Declarer has seven, but could declarer garner an overtrick? North-South +90 was a top for East-West. Even allowing declarer +120 was a reasonable score, as there were so many 150s. One board proves nothing, of course, but this is a common enough situation and a passive approach is usually best.

Tip 63 (b): Against 1NT or 2NT openings or 3NT reached after an invitational auction, be very reluctant to lead from a 4-card suit with only one honour. Even with two honours a 4-card suit can be risky without significant compensating gain. To lead from three or four rags is usually safer than from such a 4-card suit.

64   Dealer West : Both vulnerable

WEST	NORTH	EAST	SOUTH
1◇	No	1♡	4♠
No	No	Dble	All pass

What would you lead as West from:

♠ 8 3   ♡ Q J 2   ◇ A J 9 5 3   ♣ K J 9

The deal arose in a Guardian Easter Tournament in London:

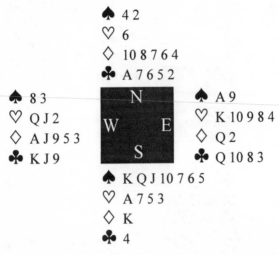

```
                    ♠ 4 2
                    ♡ 6
                    ◇ 10 8 7 6 4
                    ♣ A 7 6 5 2
      ♠ 8 3              N           ♠ A 9
      ♡ Q J 2                        ♡ K 10 9 8 4
      ◇ A J 9 5 3    W       E       ◇ Q 2
      ♣ K J 9            S           ♣ Q 10 8 3
                    ♠ K Q J 10 7 6 5
                    ♡ A 7 5 3
                    ◇ K
                    ♣ 4
```

As you have all suits covered, the trump lead can minimise any potential ruffs in dummy. Second choice would be the ◇A to take a look at dummy and then decide how best to continue. After a trump lead to the ace and a trump back, the defence should collect 500.

West was the legendary Rixi Markus, who reported the deal against herself. 'I am shamed to say,' wrote Rixi, 'that at the table I made the dreadful lead of the ♡Q. Two heart ruffs in dummy gave the fortunate declarer ten tricks.' It is a comfort to us mere mortals that superstars can also fall from grace from time to time and are big enough to admit it.

Tip 64: When your side is strong in every suit outside trumps, a trump lead is often best.

65   The opposition bidding goes 1♣ : 1♠, 3♠ : 4♠. What would you lead against 4♠ from:

♠ 8 6 3   ♡ A 10 9 4   ◊ Q 7   ♣ J 7 3 2

Auctions that start 1-minor : 1-major, 3-major are frequently based on opener's having 4-card support for responder plus a 5-card or longer minor. That is not a certainty – declarer could be 4-4-4-1 or have a strong, balanced hand type – but the long minor with opener is common enough. Whenever dummy is expected to hold a good, long suit and you are not strong in that suit, it pays to lead an unbid suit. Declarer's strategy on such hands is to draw trumps and use the long suit for discards. Unless your tricks come quickly, they may not come at all. Even though an unbid suit may be a risky choice, take the risk when dummy has a long, useful suit.

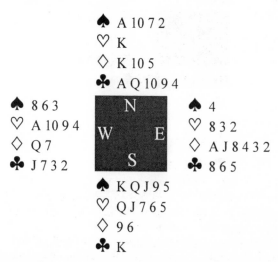

♠ A 10 7 2
♡ K
◊ K 10 5
♣ A Q 10 9 4

<table>
<tr><td>♠ 8 6 3
♡ A 10 9 4
◊ Q 7
♣ J 7 3 2</td><td>N
W   E
S</td><td>♠ 4
♡ 8 3 2
◊ A J 8 4 3 2
♣ 8 6 5</td></tr>
</table>

♠ K Q J 9 5
♡ Q J 7 6 5
◊ 9 6
♣ K

On the actual deal you needed to start with the ◊Q or the ♡A followed by a diamond switch. On a spade or a club lead, declarer will use the clubs to eliminate the diamond losers. You cannot afford a passive lead such as a trump when dummy has shown a long suit.

Tip 65: When the opposition bidding starts 1-minor : 1-major, 3-major or 4-major, leading an unbid suit is often best.

66 With only North-South vulnerable, South dealt and opened 1◇. North responded 1♡, South rebid 1NT, showing 15-17 points, and everyone passed.

What would you lead as West from:

♠ J 7 4   ♡ Q 9 8 7 6 3   ◇ 2   ♣ J 6 4

West has no attractive lead. Hearts are out : they were bid by dummy. A singleton diamond, declarer's suit, would be the last choice. That leaves it between J-x-x in the black suits.

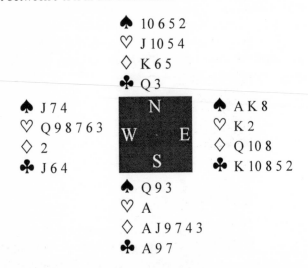

```
                ♠ 10 6 5 2
                ♡ J 10 5 4
                ◇ K 6 5
                ♣ Q 3

    ♠ J 7 4              ♠ A K 8
    ♡ Q 9 8 7 6 3        ♡ K 2
    ◇ 2                  ◇ Q 10 8
    ♣ J 6 4             ♣ K 10 8 5 2

                ♠ Q 9 3
                ♡ A
                ◇ A J 9 7 4 3
                ♣ A 9 7
```

South made a pairs decision to rebid 1NT rather than show the long diamonds. Normally, with no other guidance, West might well choose to lead the major rather than the minor, but here there was sufficient evidence to the contrary. South had shown 15-17 points and North could be placed with about 5-7 points. That gives North-South a range of 20-24 points and West was looking at just 4 HCP. West could therefore place East with 12 HCP or more.

This had become a textbook situation. After (1◇) : No : (1♡), why had East kept quiet? With five spades, East would have overcalled. With four spades, East might well have made a takeout double, especially as East was marked with heart shortage.

All the evidence pointed to East having minor suit length and so West chose the ♣4 lead. Declarer tried the queen from dummy, covered by the king. South ducked. East returned a low club, ducked to the jack, and the third club knocked out the ace. When declarer mispicked the diamonds by playing ◇K, ◇A, he was in deep trouble. East won the third diamond, West having pitched two hearts on the diamonds, and cashed the ♠K, discouraged by West. East then cashed two club winners, West discarding two more hearts. This position remained:

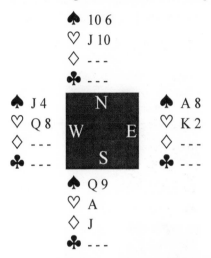

```
              ♠  10 6
              ♡  J 10
              ◇  - - -
              ♣  - - -
  ♠ J 4                      ♠ A 8
  ♡ Q 8          N           ♡ K 2
  ◇ - - -     W     E        ◇ - - -
  ♣ - - -         S          ♣ - - -
              ♠  Q 9
              ♡  A
              ◇  J
              ♣  - - -
```

Forced to hold on to ♠Q-x, South had to let go two diamond winners. A low heart now endplayed South and the defence scored the last two tricks for two down and +100. In the final of a 2003 national pairs championship, that was a shared top with one other pair. Most North-South pairs were scoring 110 in a diamond part-score.

Tip 66: When you are very weak and partner is marked with enough strength to take some action, but did not do so, ask yourself why partner has kept silent. The answer may point you towards the best lead.

67　　Dealer North : Both vulnerable

WEST	NORTH	EAST	SOUTH
	No	1♡	1♠
2♡	4♣ (1)	Dble	4♠
Dble	No	No	Rdble
No	No	No	

(1) Fit-jump: 5+ clubs and spade support as well

What would you lead as West from:

♠ 9 8 2　♡ Q 8 5 2　♢ A 9 7 6　♣ K 6

They say that those of us who do not live beyond our means simply suffer from a lack of imagination. Bridge players who live beyond their high-card means are exercising their imagination in the play of the cards. When they undertake a contract clearly not supported by high card values, lead a trump at every opportunity. If their tricks are not coming from high cards, they expect to make them by ruffing.

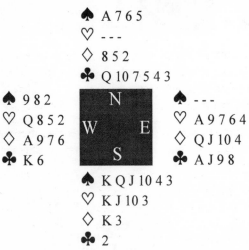

```
              ♠ A 7 6 5
              ♡ - - -
              ♢ 8 5 2
              ♣ Q 10 7 5 4 3
♠ 9 8 2                        ♠ - - -
♡ Q 8 5 2        N             ♡ A 9 7 6 4
♢ A 9 7 6    W       E         ♢ Q J 10 4
♣ K 6            S             ♣ A J 9 8
              ♠ K Q J 10 4 3
              ♡ K J 10 3
              ♢ K 3
              ♣ 2
```

A spade lead ensures one down. After the actual ♡2 lead, ruffed, a low club from dummy was won by East, who switched to the ♢Q, king, ace. When West returned a low diamond, declarer could cross-ruff for ten tricks.

Tip 67: If they bid beyond their high card values, lead a trump.

68   When declarer bids two suits and dummy gives a preference to declarer's first suit, dummy may well have more cards in declarer's first suit than in the second. If dummy prefers declarer's second suit, such as an auction like 1♠ : 1NT, 2◇ : No, dummy is bound to have greater length in the second suit. With equal length, dummy would revert to declarer's first suit. If you have potential winners in the first suit, it may pay you to lead trumps at every opportunity. This reduces dummy's ruffing potential and improves your chances of scoring your winners in declarer's side suit.

Consider this problem:

WEST	EAST	W	N	E	S
♠ 5	♠ A 9 7 6 4	1◇	No	1♠	No
♡ 2	♡ Q 10 5 3	2♣	No	2NT	No
◇ A Q 10 9 6 3	◇ 2	3♣	No	5♣	All pass
♣ K Q 8 7 6	♣ A 4 3				

North leads the ♣10. How should West plan the play?

You can scarcely afford to draw trumps. You are bound to lose one heart and while it is possible to play the diamonds for just one loser after trumps have been drawn, that would be very lucky. There is evidence that the diamonds will not be friendly. What is the clue?

On the auction a heart lead, the unbid suit, would seem attractive. What can you deduce from North's choice of a trump lead?

When a defender leads a trump after declarer has bid two suits, that defender is often strong in declarer's second suit. On the basis that North is likely to be strong in diamonds because of the trump lead, a good plan is to win with the ♣K, cash the ◇A and lead the ◇Q. You expect North to hold the ◇K.

Suppose that North plays low smoothly on the ◇Q, do you ruff this or let the ◇Q run?

Be prepared to back your judgement and let the ◇Q run, discarding a spade from dummy. The ◇Q holds the trick. On the third diamond, North plays the ◇K. How do you plan the play from here?

On the actual deal, declarer won out after a tough tussle:

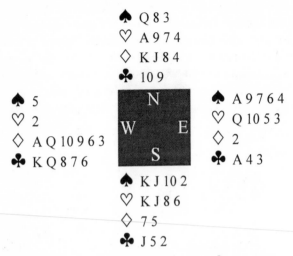

♠ Q 8 3
♡ A 9 7 4
◇ K J 8 4
♣ 10 9

♠ 5
♡ 2
◇ A Q 10 9 6 3
♣ K Q 8 7 6

♠ A 9 7 6 4
♡ Q 10 5 3
◇ 2
♣ A 4 3

♠ K J 10 2
♡ K J 8 6
◇ 7 5
♣ J 5 2

The good news for declarer from the ♣10 lead is that trumps are likely to break. Defenders rarely lead trumps when they split 4-1. The bad news is that the diamonds are likely to lie badly.

After the ♣10, taken by the ♣K, the ◇A cashed and the ◇Q led, if North had covered, declarer would have ruffed low, cashed the ♣A and the ♠A and ruffed a spade, drawn the last trump and conceded a diamond to the jack. This loses just one heart and one diamond.

When North cunningly ducked the ◇Q, declarer trusted his own analysis and let the ◇Q run. On the next diamond, North followed with the ◇K, but declarer ruffed with the ♣A. Just as well, for a low ruff in dummy would see South over-ruff and return a trump. That would leave declarer with another diamond to lose as well as a heart.

Next came the ♠A, spade ruff, diamond ruff. South declined to over-ruff, but declarer was in control: spade ruff, ♣Q and then diamond winners. Whether South ruffed or not, declarer lost only one heart and one club.

Tip 68: When declarer has bid two suits and you are strong in the non-trump suit, a trump lead will often work well.

69 Dealer East : Nil vulnerable

WEST	NORTH	EAST	SOUTH
		No	1NT
No	2♣	Dble (1)	Rdble
No	No	2♠	Dble
No	2NT	All pass	

(1) Lead-directing for clubs

What would you lead as West from:

♠ K 10 6 4   ♡ Q 7 4 3   ◇ A 10 3 2   ♣ 7

The deal arose in the final of a national pairs championship in 2003:

Because the opening lead is so vital at pairs East doubled 2♣ for the lead. When South redoubled, East prudently ran to 2♠. South doubled 2♠ for penalties, but North ran to 2NT, wisely as 2♠ is unbeatable.

Judging from the bidding that South would be strong in spades and East should be strong in clubs, West led the ♣7. East won and shifted to the ♠9. South ducked (♠A would save a trick) and shortly after the contract was two down for a 70% score to East-West.

Tip 69: When partner shows two suits, try to judge which is likely to be the stronger suit and lead that one.

70   Dealer West : Nil vulnerable

WEST	NORTH	EAST	SOUTH
No	2♢ (1)	No	No
3♣	No	3♠	No
3NT	No	No	No

(1) 10-15 HCP, 6+ diamonds, no 4-card major

What would you lead as North from:

♠ K 4   ♡ 10   ♢ A Q J 7 5 3 2   ♣ 9 8 3

With a sure entry you could start with ♢A, ♢Q, but the ♠K may not be an entry. To start with the ♢Q is risky. Partner may not have a second diamond. It is attractive to try to find partner's entry to have a diamond lead come through declarer and that is why North chose the ♡10 lead in the 1988 Olympiad. This was the full deal:

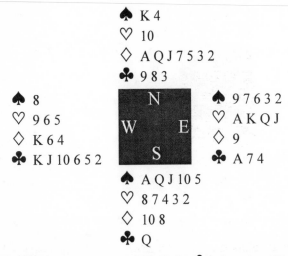

The ♡10 was not a success. With the ♣Q dropping, West had ten tricks. The culprit was South, who had a lapse of concentration, something one cannot afford, especially at pairs. South should have doubled 3♠ to show strength there and indicate a spade lead to North. After a spade lead, North-South can take twelve tricks. East-West may now avoid 3NT, but that will be better for North-South than the actual result.

Tip 70 (a): Be quick to double if that tells partner what to lead.

Dealer East : Nil vulnerable

WEST	NORTH	EAST	SOUTH
		No	1♡
2NT (1)	4♢ (2)	?	

(1) Weak, both minors
(2) Heart support, game-force, ♢A, no ♣A

What action should East take with:

♠ K J 6 4 3   ♡ 5 3   ♢ 8 4   ♣ J 5 4 2

From your paltry values the opponents will probably bid to slam. You could bid 5♣, but you do not want a club lead. Partner is unlikely to have two defensive tricks. A spade lead is your only hope for a defensive trick, but you need to make that clear to partner.

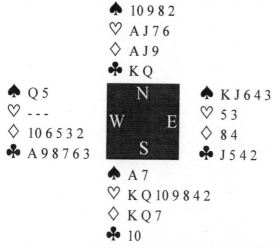

        ♠ 10 9 8 2
        ♡ A J 7 6
        ♢ A J 9
        ♣ K Q

♠ Q 5   ♠ K J 6 4 3
♡ - - -   N   ♡ 5 3
♢ 10 6 5 3 2   W   E   ♢ 8 4
♣ A 9 8 7 6 3   S   ♣ J 5 4 2

        ♠ A 7
        ♡ K Q 10 9 8 4 2
        ♢ K Q 7
        ♣ 10

In the 1989 Staten Bank Invitation Tournament, Billy Eisenberg (USA) and Tony Forrester (Great Britain) both made the excellent 4♠ bid, intending to run to 5♣ if doubled. Undaunted, both Souths continued with 4NT and bid 6♡ after the reply. After the ♠Q lead each time, 6♡ was one down. Without a spade lead the slam would have made.

Tip 70 (b): If you intend to sacrifice or it is not clear which side can make what, make a lead-directing bid if partner is on lead and the expected lead is unlikely to be best for your side.

71   Dealer South : North-South vulnerable

WEST	NORTH	EAST	SOUTH
			1♠
No	4♢ (1)	No	4NT
No	5♢ (2)	No	5♡ (3)
No	5♠ (4)	All pass	

(1) Splinter raise of spades, values for game, short in diamonds
(2) One key card for spades, either an ace or the ♠K
(3) Asking for the queen of trumps
(4) Denies the ♠Q

What would you lead as West from:

♠ 7   ♡ Q 7 3   ♢ 10 8 7 6 4 3   ♣ J 9 2

What would your answer be if East had doubled 4♢?

There are two schools of thought about how best to play the double of a splinter bid. One view is that it shows length and strength in the splinter suit and suggests a sacrifice. The other view is that the double is more useful to indicate a specific lead.

The opportunities for doubling to suggest a sacrifice are rare. Sometimes the vulnerability will be wrong for a sacrifice, on other occasions you might have defensive prospects and finally, you cannot yet be sure whether a sacrifice is indicated as you do not know how high the opponents plan to bid. You could be willing to sacrifice against their game, but not if they push themselves to a slam. As partner cannot know this, partner might take a phantom sacrifice against their slam if you double their splinter, while you were happy to defend.

Doubling for a sacrifice has adherents because there is little value in doubling to ask for a lead of the splinter suit. As dummy will have a singleton or void in that suit, your side can score one trick there at best. Even worse, if the double reveals that your side has strength in the short suit, this may persuade the opponents that they have few wasted values in this suit and therefore push on to a good slam.

These days many pairs have adopted the idea suggested by George Rosenkranz of Mexico to use the double of a splinter as lead-directing. The double, however, asks for the lead of some other suit.

Rosenkranz suggested the double asks for the lead of the suit *below* the splinter suit in rank. If that happens to be the trump suit, go to the next suit down. Another popular style today is that the double asks for the higher-ranking non-trump suit outside the splinter.

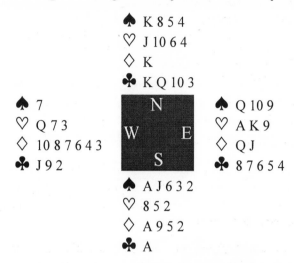

♠ K 8 5 4
♡ J 10 6 4
◇ K
♣ K Q 10 3

♠ 7
♡ Q 7 3
◇ 10 8 7 6 4 3
♣ J 9 2

♠ Q 10 9
♡ A K 9
◇ Q J
♣ 8 7 6 5 4

♠ A J 6 3 2
♡ 8 5 2
◇ A 9 5 2
♣ A

East-West were using the Rosenkranz formula where a double of 4◇ would have asked for a club lead. When the bidding subsided in 5♠, West judged that East's failure to double suggested that East was more interested in a heart lead than a club. West led a heart and the defence speedily cashed three hearts. When declarer misguessed the spades later, that was two down.

At other tables, with less information, West often led a diamond and declarer was able to discard all the heart losers for a huge score. North's splinter is not a textbook example, but the bridge world is full of players whose bids do not resemble textbook recommendations.

Using the double to ask for the high-ranking suit, East would double 4◇ to ask for a heart lead. The more lead-directing bids you have in your arsenal, the more often you can indicate the lead you feel is best.

Tip 71: Make sure you have a clear understanding with your partner what to expect when you double a splinter bid.

72   After East passed as dealer, South opened 1♣, West overcalled 1♡ and North bid 1♠.   South reversed with 2♢, North bid 3♣, non-forcing preference, and South bid 3NT, passed out.

What would you lead as West from:

♠ K 8 7 4   ♡ Q 10 8 5 3   ♢ A 8   ♣ 7 4

The natural lead against 3NT is from your long suit. Is there any reason to depart from the heart lead?

Partner probably lacks three hearts (failure to support hearts). Further, declarer has shown 5+ clubs and 4+ diamonds, and then shown at least one heart stopper with 3NT. Declarer's pattern is likely to be 1=3=4=5 and so perhaps spades is the weak spot for North-South.

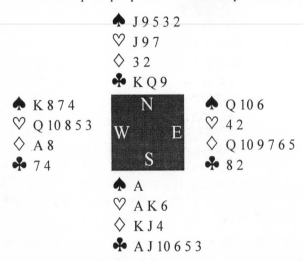

♠ J 9 5 3 2
♡ J 9 7
♢ 3 2
♣ K Q 9

♠ K 8 7 4   ♠ Q 10 6
♡ Q 10 8 5 3   ♡ 4 2
♢ A 8   ♢ Q 10 9 7 6 5
♣ 7 4   ♣ 8 2

♠ A
♡ A K 6
♢ K J 4
♣ A J 10 6 5 3

In the semi-final of the 2001 European Open Pairs most declarers made eleven tricks after a heart lead via a diamond to the jack. Christian Mari, France, led the ♠4 and Alain Levy, East, played the ♠6. Declarer won with the ace and rattled off six rounds of clubs. West was under pressure but, knowing the spade position, was able to pitch two hearts, the ♠7 and the ♠K. South was now held to nine tricks.

Tip 72: If declarer shows length in two suits and a stopper in the third suit, declarer is likely to be short in the remaining suit.

73   Dealer South : East-West vulnerable

WEST	NORTH	EAST	SOUTH
			No
1♠	2NT (1)	3♡	5♣
Double	No	No	No

(1) Weak, both minors

What would you lead as West from:

♠ A J 9 8 4 3   ♡ Q J 6   ◇ J 9 7   ♣ A

When the opponents are sacrificing and you have no standout lead, leading an ace can be useful. Once you see dummy, the path ahead may be clearer. Leading the singleton ace of trumps is unlikely to cost. The deal is from a national championship in 2001:

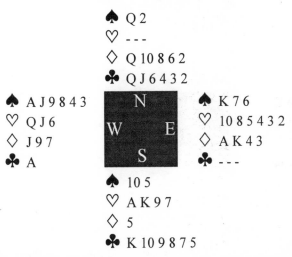

```
                  ♠ Q 2
                  ♡ - - -
                  ◇ Q 10 8 6 2
                  ♣ Q J 6 4 3 2
 ♠ A J 9 8 4 3         N          ♠ K 7 6
 ♡ Q J 6       W           E      ♡ 10 8 5 4 3 2
 ◇ J 9 7                          ◇ A K 4 3
 ♣ A               S              ♣ - - -
                  ♠ 10 5
                  ♡ A K 9 7
                  ◇ 5
                  ♣ K 10 9 8 7 5
```

South's initial pass is very conservative in this day and age. If you lead the ♣A, the switch to ace and another spade is obvious and you collect +500. The same happens, a touch luckily, on the ♠A lead. That may not have been so rosy if dummy were void in spades and declarer had ♠K-Q-x and an entry. On the ♡Q lead, you will soon be writing minus 750 on the score-sheet for a likely bottom board.

Tip 73: Leading ace singleton in the trump suit can often be a good start against a sacrifice.

74   Dealer South : East-West vulnerable

WEST	NORTH	EAST	SOUTH
			4♢
No	No	Dble*	All pass

*For takeout

What would you lead as West from:

♠ K 9 4   ♡ Q 9 3   ♢ 8 7 5   ♣ 7 6 4 3

With a 4-3-3-3 pattern it is not attractive to reply to a high-level takeout double. Prefer to pass and defend. At this vulnerability East should have a strong hand and 4♢ is likely to fail.

The deal arose in a national championship in 2003:

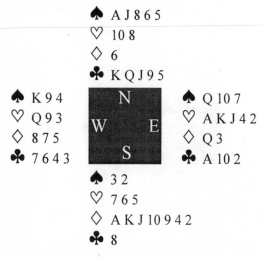

East's shape for the double is not ideal, but a problem will arise only if West bids or finds the wrong lead. As East should be prepared for a bid in either major, try a major suit lead. Choose a spade, as it is usually better to lead from a king than a queen. A spade lead and trump switch gives you +300. A heart lead and a spade switch will achieve the same. A trump lead or two rounds of hearts followed by a trump switch gives you +100, while a club lead allows 4♢ to make.

Tip 74: When partner has shown all round strength, it is usually safer to lead from a king-high suit than one headed by the queen.

75   Dealer South : Both vulnerable

WEST	NORTH	EAST	SOUTH
			4♠
Dble*	No	No	No

*For takeout

What would you lead as West from:

♠ 5   ♡ A K J 9 6   ◇ 9 5 2   ♣ A K 7 4

Although your double is primarily for takeout, partner has elected to play for penalties. With those luscious A-K suits it's just a matter of how many down, right? So which A-K suit do you choose?

In the final of a national championship in 2001, there were several red faces among the East-West pairs after this deal:

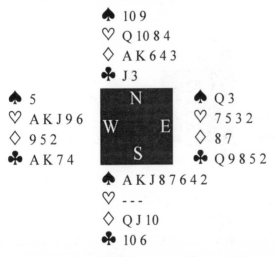

```
              ♠ 10 9
              ♡ Q 10 8 4
              ◇ A K 6 4 3
              ♣ J 3
♠ 5                          ♠ Q 3
♡ A K J 9 6        N         ♡ 7 5 3 2
◇ 9 5 2        W     E       ◇ 8 7
♣ A K 7 4          S         ♣ Q 9 8 5 2
              ♠ A K J 8 7 6 4 2
              ♡ - - -
              ◇ Q J 10
              ♣ 10 6
```

There is no lead to beat 5♠, let alone 4♠ doubled. Best is to cash two clubs, giving South +990. Lead a top heart and you share a bottom with –1390. It is true that clubs might be 4-0 and hearts 2-2, but with only your own cards to guide you, declarer is likely to be shorter in your long suit. Note how much better it is if East does take out the double.

Tip 75: With a choice of two equally strong leads against a trump contract, choose the lead in the shorter suit.

76   With only East-West vulnerable, South dealt and opened 1♡. West doubled, North jumped to 3♡ and South's 4♡ was passed out. What would you lead as West from:

♠ A J 6 3   ♡ 9   ◇ A 5 4 3   ♣ Q 9 8 4

With no obviously good lead, start by eliminating the terrible leads. The worst lead against a trump contract is almost always the lead of an unsupported ace. A singleton trump might trap a potential winner with partner and so you are left with only the clubs, not an appealing start but not nearly as awful as the other choices.

In the 2001 Portuguese Pairs, reported by Patrick Jourdain in the IBPA Bulletin, West led the ♡9 and paid a terrible price.

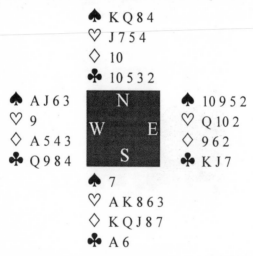

```
                    ♠ K Q 8 4
                    ♡ J 7 5 4
                    ◇ 10
                    ♣ 10 5 3 2

   ♠ A J 6 3           N           ♠ 10 9 5 2
   ♡ 9                             ♡ Q 10 2
   ◇ A 5 4 3      W       E        ◇ 9 6 2
   ♣ Q 9 8 4           S           ♣ K J 7

                    ♠ 7
                    ♡ A K 8 6 3
                    ◇ K Q J 8 7
                    ♣ A 6
```

Declarer, Jason Hackett of England, played the ♡J and captured the ♡Q. He then led the ◇7 and West took another tumble, playing second hand low (how many diamond tricks was he expecting the defence to take?). The ◇10 won and next came ♡4 – two – eight. The last trump was drawn and declarer made +480, losing just one trick to the ♠A, for an absolute top. On a club lead, unless declarer picks the heart position (not too likely), the contract will go one down.

Tip 76: Avoid leading unsupported aces against a suit contract and you need strong evidence to justify a singleton trump lead.

77   Dealer North : Both vulnerable

WEST	NORTH	EAST	SOUTH
	1◇	No	1♠
No	2NT (1)	No	4♠
No	No	No	

(1) 19-20 balanced, forcing to game

What would you lead as West from:

♠ A J 7   ♡ K J 9 7   ◇ J 2   ♣ 10 5 3 2

Declarer has shown 6+ spades and dummy has a strong balanced hand. With no evidence that dummy will give declarer discards, there is no urgency for an attacking lead. Each of your suits is a risky lead, but the club suit is the least risky. The deal arose in the 1980 Olympiad:

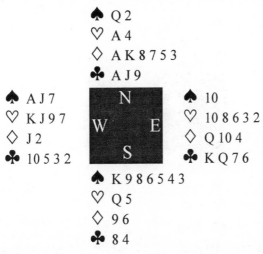

At one table Bobby Wolff led the ♡7, ending any chance to beat the contract. Tim Seres ducked it to the queen and played a spade to the queen and another spade. He lost two spades and a club. +620. At the other table the lead was the ♣2 – nine – queen. East switched to a heart and declarer was one down. Although this arose in a teams match, the principle is even more appropriate for pairs.

Tip 77: When dummy has shown a strong, balanced hand, there is no rush to make an attacking lead.

78 With only North-South vulnerable, East passed and South opened 1NT (15-17). North bid 2♢ (transfer to hearts) and South jumped to 3♡ (maximum with four trumps). North's 4♡ was passed out.

What would you lead as West from:

♠ K J 8 4   ♡ 10   ♢ 10 6 4 3 2   ♣ 5 3 2

Dummy has shown five hearts and no length in any other suit. Declarer has shown a balanced hand. In such situations, there is no rush to make an attacking lead. Better to lead from a useless suit than to lead away from a single honour or a broken honour holding. That eliminates spades. The singleton trump is also a risky start (what if partner has Q-x-x?). The clubs are slightly safer than the diamonds where your holding is headed by an honour, the 10.

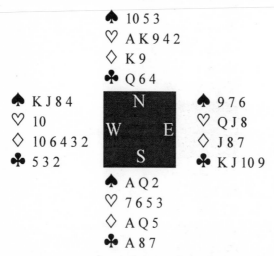

	♠ 10 5 3	
	♡ A K 9 4 2	
	♢ K 9	
	♣ Q 6 4	
♠ K J 8 4		♠ 9 7 6
♡ 10		♡ Q J 8
♢ 10 6 4 3 2		♢ J 8 7
♣ 5 3 2		♣ K J 10 9
	♠ A Q 2	
	♡ 7 6 5 3	
	♢ A Q 5	
	♣ A 8 7	

After a minor suit lead, 4♡ will probably go one down as both black kings are wrong. Even a trump lead does not hurt this time, but on a spade lead, 4♡ will succeed. In a major championship in 2001, no pairs found 3NT, usually the best spot with a 5-3-3-2 opposite a 4-3-3-3 (see Tip 14).

Tip 78: With no obviously good lead, choose a passive lead if there is no evidence of a good, long suit in dummy outside trumps.

79 With only East-West vulnerable, South deals and North-South have an unimpeded auction: 1♥ : 1♠, 2♣ : 3♣, 3♠ : 5♣, No.

What would you lead as West from:

♠ 10 8 6　♥ Q　◇ K Q 10 9 7 6 2　♣ 6 3

If you can trust their bidding South will have a singleton or void in diamonds. South has bid two suits and shown delayed support for a third suit. South's most likely hand pattern is 3-5-1-4. The safe lead is the diamond. This will not gain any tricks but will not cost any either.

The ♥Q is not a silly choice. It would fall on the first round of hearts anyway. Leading the ♥Q may also mislead declarer as to the location of the ♥J. Partner almost certainly has five hearts and, as both black suits are behaving, a ruff may be essential to score well.

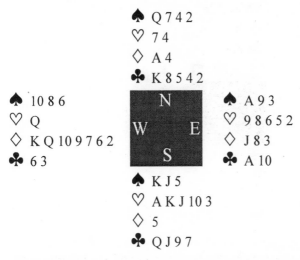

```
              ♠ Q 7 4 2
              ♥ 7 4
              ◇ A 4
              ♣ K 8 5 4 2
♠ 10 8 6          N          ♠ A 9 3
♥ Q                          ♥ 9 8 6 5 2
◇ K Q 10 9 7 6 2  W    E     ◇ J 8 3
♣ 6 3             S          ♣ A 10
              ♠ K J 5
              ♥ A K J 10 3
              ◇ 5
              ♣ Q J 9 7
```

The deal arose in the 2000 Olympiad. At the vulnerability, as East-West are unlikely to win the auction, West's silence is reasonable.

After a diamond lead, declarer has an easy path to eleven tricks and +400. A heart lead will produce a heart ruff and 5♣ goes one down.

Tip 79: If you are very weak and partner is marked with strength, leading a singleton in declarer's suit may be the best chance.

80	WEST	NORTH	EAST	SOUTH
Dealer North		No	1♢	No
Nil vulnerable	1♠	Dble	No	2♣
	No	No	2♠	3♣
	No	No	Dble	All pass

What would you lead as West from:

♠ Q J 9 7   ♡ 9 6 4   ♢ Q J 7   ♣ 9 8 6

Partner cannot have a trump stack but has suggested penalties. As East cannot expect to score enough tricks in spades and diamonds, East has to be strong in hearts. Declarer thus figures to be short in hearts and may well be planning a cross-ruff. That strongly suggests a trump lead.

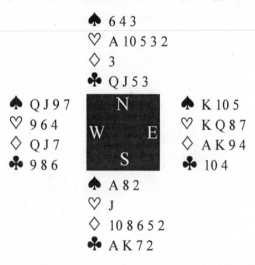

```
            ♠ 6 4 3
            ♡ A 10 5 3 2
            ♢ 3
            ♣ Q J 5 3
♠ Q J 9 7       N        ♠ K 10 5
♡ 9 6 4                  ♡ K Q 8 7
♢ Q J 7     W       E    ♢ A K 9 4
♣ 9 8 6         S        ♣ 10 4
            ♠ A 8 2
            ♡ J
            ♢ 10 8 6 5 2
            ♣ A K 7 2
```

At teams or rubber East would not dream of doubling 3♣, but the pairs game is replete with tight doubles. In the final of the 2002 World Open Pairs, West led the ♢Q. East overtook and shifted to a trump, but it was too late. Declarer could now cross-ruff for +470 and a 95% score. After a trump lead and another trump when in with a diamond, the defence can hold declarer to eight tricks for +100 and an 80% score to East-West.

Tip 80: Where a cross-ruff is threatened, start with a trump lead and continue with trumps at each opportunity.

Part 4: DECLARER PLAY

The bidding is over, the lead appears, dummy comes down. This is the moment when good habits can bear fruit. Before you play any card, stop and count dummy's HCP and your own. Then estimate where the missing points are likely to be and whether you are in a poor contract, the normal spot or an excellent contract. This can have an important bearing on how to tackle the play.

At rubber or teams your task is to make your contract, whether the contract is good, bad or routine. At pairs, the story is quite different. Suppose you find yourself in 3NT and see that 4♡ is the normal contract. If ten tricks are comfortable there, you cannot be satisfied with just nine tricks in 3NT. You must go all out to score the tenth trick in 3NT notwithstanding the risk. If 3NT making is a rotten score, 3NT failing will not be much worse. By risking the contract for the overtrick, you are risking only a little in order to gain a lot. Such thinking is the heart and soul of pairs play.

You judge that your contract is normal. Next consider their opening lead. Does it appear to be the usual lead? Was it made swiftly or only after long deliberation? A quick lead means the same lead is likely at other tables. A slow lead means that other tables may fare better or worse. If the lead does not appear to be automatic and has given you an extra trick, make sure you retain the edge received. If the lead is not automatic and looks ominous, you may have to take chances to recover the ground lost.

If you feel your contract is superb, you should take no chances at all. If doubled, making your contract will usually be enough to ensure an excellent score. The same applies to a slam you feel the rest of the field will not reach. Safety plays which involve conceding a trick to guard against a bad break usually cannot be afforded at pairs. In a doubled contract or an uncommon slam, be prepared to concede a trick if that makes your contract certain or more likely.

If doubled in a part-score not vulnerable, your aim may be to ensure one down, −100, and not two down for −300 and a terrible score.

WEST	EAST	W	N	E	S
♠ K Q 9 6 4 3	♠ A J			1♣	No
♡ Q J 3	♡ K 9 4 2	1♠	2♢	No	No
♢ 10 8 3 2	♢ 9 7	2♠	No	3♠	No
♣ - - -	♣ A K 5 3 2	4♠	No	No	No

North starts with the ♢A: 7 – 5 – 3 and continues with the ♢K, South following with the ♢Q. North continues with the ♢6. You ruff with the ♠A and South plays the ♣4. What now?

4♠ is an excellent spot and may not be reached at all tables. Making 4♠ will be a very good score, but one off will be a shared bottom. Therefore strive to ensure the contract and do not seek an overtrick.

Continue with ♠J, ♣A, pitching a diamond, ruff a club and cash ♠K, ♠Q. If trumps are 3-2 you are home and would be on the actual deal:

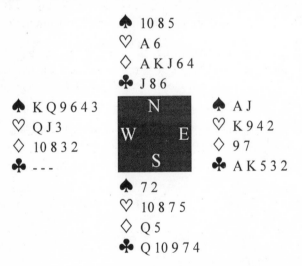

```
              ♠ 10 8 5
              ♡ A 6
              ♢ A K J 6 4
              ♣ J 8 6
♠ K Q 9 6 4 3      N        ♠ A J
♡ Q J 3                     ♡ K 9 4 2
♢ 10 8 3 2     W     E      ♢ 9 7
♣ - - -                     ♣ A K 5 3 2
                   S
              ♠ 7 2
              ♡ 10 8 7 5
              ♢ Q 5
              ♣ Q 10 9 7 4
```

If you err by playing a heart at trick 4, North will win and play a fourth diamond. That gives the defence a trump trick and you are one down.

Tip 81: Do not jeopardise a good score for the sake of an overtrick.

WEST	EAST	W	N	E	S
♠ A K 4	♠ Q 5	2NT	No	3◇	No
♡ A 8 3	♡ K Q 10 9 6 4	3♡	No	4NT	No
◇ A Q J 3	◇ 7 2	5♣	No	5NT	No
♣ K 8 3	♣ A 6 2	6♡	No	No	No

3◇ = transfer to hearts; 5♣ = 0 or 3 key cards for hearts; 6♡ = two kings outside hearts. North leads the ♣J. Plan your play.

The first thing to realise is that you are in a dreadful contract. Your partner has obviously learned all the gadgets (such as transfers and Roman Key Card Blackwood), but not enough about basic strategy at pairs. You belong in 6NT, of course, together with almost every other pair. With 31-32 HCP plus a running suit, the field should be in 6NT.

No point worrying about that now. What will happen in 6NT? There are twelve top tricks (play the ♡K first just in case they do break 4-0) and those in 6NT will try the diamond finesse for the thirteenth trick.

Your only hope for a good score is that the diamond finesse fails. If the ◇K is with South, those in 6NT make thirteen tricks and you cannot beat that score. If the ◇K is with North, those in 6NT make twelve tricks and you still cannot beat their score if you play South for the ◇K.

Take the ♣A, draw trumps, cash the spades and discard a diamond from dummy on the third spade. You continue with the ◇A, then ◇Q to take a ruffing finesse. If North plays low, you let the ◇Q run.

If South has the ◇K, you make twelve tricks while those in 6NT make thirteen, but that is immaterial. You could never beat them. However, if North has the ◇K, you will make thirteen tricks, while those in 6NT make just twelve. The trouble with your top score is that partner's bidding may not improve.

Tip 82: If you are in an inferior spot which will score less than the normal spot, take a line of play which may not be available in the normal contract, but which provides a better score if successful.

Dealer East : Both vulnerable

WEST	EAST	W	N	E	S
♠ Q J 6 4 2	♠ A K 7 3			1♣	No
♡ K 8 3	♡ 9 4	1♠	No	2♠	No
◇ A 7 6	◇ Q 5	4♠	No	No	No
♣ Q 7	♣ A J 10 4 2				

Lead: ♡Q. South takes the ♡A and switches to the ◇2. Plan the play.

A novice defender may hand you a gift from time to time. A good defender will not. Where a defender makes a switch, which looks like it is handing you an extra trick, it is pounds to peanuts that the card that 'could be right' will be wrong. If you have a sensible alternative play for the same extra trick, it will usually pay you to take that play.

There are many such situations and defenders tend not to lead away from honours where a significant risk exists. If dummy has J-x, a defender will normally not lead away from the queen. Likewise, if dummy has Q-x, a defender is unlikely to lead away from the king.

Although a switch to diamonds looks normal for South here, do not expect South to have the ◇K. If you duck, North will win with the ◇K and you will make ten tricks if the club finesse loses or eleven tricks if North has the ♣K.

By taking the ◇A at trick 2, you might make twelve tricks. Draw trumps in two or three rounds, ending in hand, and then tackle the clubs by leading the ♣Q. If North started with ♣K-x-x, you obtain two discards from dummy and both your diamond losers can be swiftly discarded. You can also make twelve tricks if North began with ♣K-x or ♣K-x-x-x. After the club finesse works and you discard one diamond on the third round of clubs, you ruff the fourth club. That sets up the fifth club for another discard and you reach dummy via a heart ruff after cashing the ♡K.

If South turns up with the ♣K you make only ten tricks. If South has the ◇K as well, congratulate South, through gritted teeth, no doubt.

Tip 83: Assume the defenders are not doing you any favours.

84   Dealer North : Nil vulnerable

WEST	EAST	W	N	E	S
♠ K J 7	♠ Q 6		No	1♣	No
♡ 10 5	♡ K J 4 2	1◇	1♠	Dble*	2◇**
◇ A Q 10 8 7 6 5	◇ K J 2	3NT	No	No	No
♣ 6	♣ K 8 5 4	*For takeout **Strong spade raise

North leads the ♠4 and dummy's queen wins. Plan your play.

You have eight tricks and need one more. You can set up the extra trick in spades, but if you do that, North will realise this must be your ninth trick. Now a club switch or even a heart switch might lay you low.

The deal arose in the finals of a national tournament in 2003:

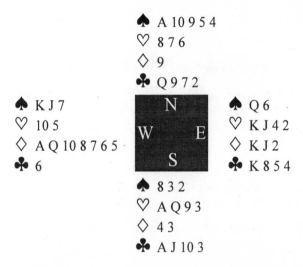

North hand:
♠ A 10 9 5 4
♡ 8 7 6
◇ 9
♣ Q 9 7 2

West hand:
♠ K J 7
♡ 10 5
◇ A Q 10 8 7 6 5
♣ 6

East hand:
♠ Q 6
♡ K J 4 2
◇ K J 2
♣ K 8 5 4

South hand:
♠ 8 3 2
♡ A Q 9 3
◇ 4 3
♣ A J 10 3

At one table declarer played a spade back at trick 2 and North ducked! They share the title, 'Naive Player of the Year'.

Australian star Paul Marston produced the right psychology. He played the ◇2 to his ace and ran the ♡10. South won and returned a spade. Here North reasonably ducked West's ♠K and 3NT was home.

Tip 84: It usually pays to mask your strength as declarer.

85 Dealer North : Nil vulnerable

WEST	EAST	W	N	E	S
♠ A 5 4	♠ K 9 8 3		No	1♢	No
♡ K 9 4	♡ A 3	3NT	No	No	No
♢ K 8 7	♢ Q 9 5 4 3				
♣ K 10 9 5	♣ A 2				

North leads the ♡6 (fourth-highest): 3 – jack – 4. South returns the
♡8: 9 – 5 – ace. How should West plan the play?

You need tricks in diamonds. You could lead a diamond to the king or
come to hand and lead a diamond towards the queen. Which shall it be?

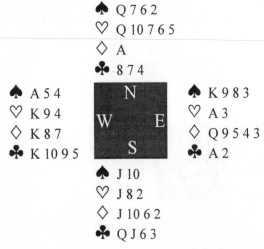

♠ Q 7 6 2
♡ Q 10 7 6 5
♢ A
♣ 8 7 4

♠ A 5 4
♡ K 9 4
♢ K 8 7
♣ K 10 9 5

♠ K 9 8 3
♡ A 3
♢ Q 9 5 4 3
♣ A 2

♠ J 10
♡ J 8 2
♢ J 10 6 2
♣ Q J 6 3

In a national tournament in the USA the popular play at trick 3 was a
diamond to the king. This turned out badly, but was motivated no doubt
by the desire not to open either of the black suits.

On the play, North has shown five hearts and South three. As North has
length in hearts, North is likely to be shorter in diamonds. That is
enough to justify coming to hand with a spade to lead a diamond
through North. You gain if North has ♢A-x and on the actual layout.

**Tip 85: If one opponent has significant length in one suit, that
player is likely to be short in another critical suit.**

Dealer East : Both vulnerable

WEST	EAST	W	N	E	S
♠ A K 9 8 7 6	♠ Q 10			No	No
♡ Q 3	♡ 7 5 4 2	1♠	No	2♢	No
♢ 5	♢ A J 9 6 2	2♠	No	3♠	No
♣ A 9 7 3	♣ K 6	4♠	No	No	No

North leads the ♡J. South takes the ♡K, ♡A and plays the ♡6 next. You ruff with the ♠6 and North has followed with the ♡8 and ♡10. How should West continue?

At teams or rubber bridge, you would play safe for ten tricks: club to the king; club to the ace; ruff a club with ♠Q; ♢A; diamond ruffed high; ruff the last club with the ♠10, losing at most two hearts and the ♠J.

Playing pairs, as your contract seems normal, you should play for eleven tricks, hoping for a normal 4-3 split in clubs.

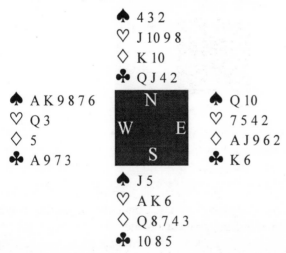

                ♠ 4 3 2
                ♡ J 10 9 8
                ♢ K 10
                ♣ Q J 4 2

♠ A K 9 8 7 6   ♠ Q 10
♡ Q 3   ♡ 7 5 4 2
♢ 5   ♢ A J 9 6 2
♣ A 9 7 3   ♣ K 6

                ♠ J 5
                ♡ A K 6
                ♢ Q 8 7 4 3
                ♣ 10 8 5

Cash ♣K, ♣A and ruff the third club with the ♠10. Then ♢A, ruff a diamond low, ruff the last club and ruff a heart or a diamond low. If this survives, play off the ♠A, ♠K. If the ♠J drops you have eleven tricks.

Tip 86: If you hold six cards or fewer between you and dummy, three rounds of the suit will usually survive without an enemy ruff.

87   To test your play, cover the East-West cards. East opened 2♠, a weak two, passed to North, who doubled. South bid 3♡ and North 4♡.

West leads the ♠9: 6 – Q – 5. East switches to the ◇5: 7 – J – A. How would you continue?

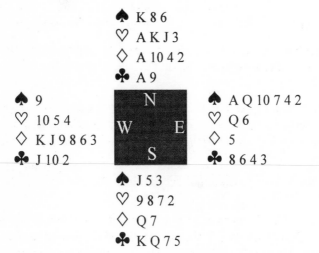

```
                    ♠ K 8 6
                    ♡ A K J 3
                    ◇ A 10 4 2
                    ♣ A 9
    ♠ 9                 N         ♠ A Q 10 7 4 2
    ♡ 10 5 4                      ♡ Q 6
    ◇ K J 9 8 6 3   W       E     ◇ 5
    ♣ J 10 2            S         ♣ 8 6 4 3
                    ♠ J 5 3
                    ♡ 9 8 7 2
                    ◇ Q 7
                    ♣ K Q 7 5
```

South cashed the ♡A, came to hand with a club and took the heart finesse. East won, cashed the ♠A and gave a West a spade ruff. West cashed the ◇K for two down, a bottom for North-South.

South needs to diagnose East's failure to continue spades when West's ♠9 was clearly a singleton or from a doubleton. East was afraid that West might have two spades and if South ruffed the third spade with the ♡10, West's failure to over-ruff would place the ♡Q with East.

Once you work that out, cash ♡A, ♡K. When the ♡Q drops, play a diamond to the queen and king without cashing the ♡J. If West shifts to a club, take the ♣A, cash the ◇10, discarding a spade, and ruff the last diamond. When East turns up with two hearts and one diamond, you can place East with six spades and four clubs. Play a heart to the jack and dummy's last heart will squeeze East in the black suits.

Tip 87: If a defender does something quite strange, stop and ask yourself why. Assume their play has an underlying logic.

WEST	EAST	W	N	E	S
♠ K	♠ A J 10 9			No	No
♡ A 9 8 7 5	♡ K 6 4 3 2	1♡	No	3♡	No
◇ A J 3	◇ 8 6	4♡	No	No	No
♣ Q J 10 9	♣ 8 5	Lead: ◇K. Plan the play.			

If you duck the ◇K, you are almost certainly limited to ten tricks. There is a good chance for eleven tricks if trumps are 2-1.

Take the ◇A, cash ♡A, ♠K and cross to the ♡K (keeping the ♡5 in hand). Discard a diamond on the ♠A and lead the ♠J. If South plays the ♠Q, ruff high, overtake the ♡5 with the ♡6, discard your other diamond on the ♠10 and ruff dummy's diamond. If South plays low on the ♠J, you can play South for the ♠Q anyway by discarding your remaining diamond or ruff high and hope the ♠Q falls from North.

After ◇A, ♡A, if trumps are 3-0, play the ♠K and overtake it with the ♠A. Then lead ♠J. If South has the ♠Q, you have a good chance to make 4♡. This line does risk going two down, but you will have company. Other strong declarers will play the same way.

WEST	EAST	W	N	E	S
♠ K 3 2	♠ A Q 9 6 5 4	1NT	No	2♡ (1)	No
♡ K 7	♡ A 3	2♠	No	4♠	All pass
◇ K 6 3 2	◇ Q J	(1) Transfer to spades			
♣ A 6 4 2	♣ 8 5 3	Lead: ♣K. Plan the play.			

If trumps are normal, then tricks are easy. At teams you would take the ♣A and draw trumps. At pairs there is a chance for eleven tricks at slight risk if you duck the first club. If North plays a second club and South does not ruff, you take the ♣A, draw trumps and play on diamonds. If the ◇A is with South and South started with only two clubs, you will be able to discard dummy's third club on the ◇K.

Tip 88: Do not hold up an ace at a trump contract without a good reason. At pairs, a potential overtrick is reason enough.

Dealer North : Nil vulnerable

WEST	EAST	W	N	E	S
♠ K Q 5 2	♠ A 4 3		No	1◇	No
♡ Q 10 8 4 2	♡ K 7 6	1♡	No	2◇	No
◇ 5	◇ A Q 6 4 3 2	2♠	No	3♡	No
♣ A J 3	♣ 4	4♡	No	No	No

North leads the ♣7 to South's queen and your ace. What next?

You should take your club ruffs before touching trumps. Ruff a club, spade to the king and ruff your third club. The ♡K next is taken by South, who plays another club. You ruff and North follows. You cash the ♡Q. Both follow, but the ♡J has not dropped. When you play a third heart, South wins with the jack and exits with a spade. How do you play from here?

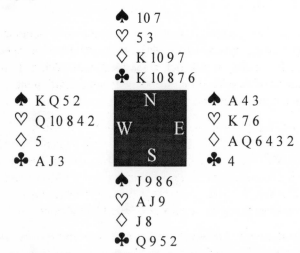

          ♠ 10 7
          ♡ 5 3
          ◇ K 10 9 7
          ♣ K 10 8 7 6

♠ K Q 5 2   ♠ A 4 3
♡ Q 10 8 4 2   ♡ K 7 6
◇ 5   ◇ A Q 6 4 3 2
♣ A J 3   ♣ 4

          ♠ J 9 8 6
          ♡ A J 9
          ◇ J 8
          ♣ Q 9 5 2

The question is whether you take the diamond finesse or play for spades to be 3-3. The diamond finesse at 50% offers the better chance and you should win with the ♠Q and finesse the ◇Q. When this wins you have a discard for your fourth spade and eleven tricks. The 3-3 spade break, originally only 36%, is less likely. Even if the diamond finesse loses, you make ten tricks as the ◇A takes care of the fourth spade.

You could back your judgement of the spade position. If you trust their signalling and they have shown an odd number of spades each, you might choose to play ♠A and back to ♠Q. If spades turn out to be 4-2, do not take the diamond finesse. If that fails, so might the contract. Making eleven tricks will be a top board, making ten will not be too bad, but going one off will be a revolting score.

After spades prove to be 4-2, play off your last two trumps. If the ♢K is with the player with four spades, that player will be squeezed and you can always play your ♢A at the end to ensure ten tricks.

WEST	EAST	North leads a club and West
♠ A K J 3	♠ 7 6 4	ruffs the second club. How
♡ K Q 9 4 3	♡ A 7 6 5 2	should West plan the play:
♢ A K J	♢ 8 7	(a) if the contract is 6♡?
♣ 8	♣ 9 3 2	(b) if the contract is 4♡?

(a) In 6♡ you should combine your chances in spades and diamonds. After drawing trumps, cash the ♠A, ♠K. If the ♠Q has dropped, you are home. If the ♠Q is still out, cross to dummy with a trump and take the diamond finesse. If that works, you can discard dummy's spade loser on the third diamond.

The chance that North has ♠Q-x is slight, about 8%, but in 6♡ that extra chance is worthwhile. 6♡ is an excellent slam, which few will reach. Making 6♡ will give you a top, while two down instead of one down will be make almost no difference, just another bottom. The extra undertrick is almost free and justifies the extra chance of making the slam, increasing your odds beyond 50% for either finesse.

(b) 4♡ will be the normal contract. This is safe for eleven tricks and you must not risk making only ten. Draw trumps and cash the ♢A, ♢K. On a lucky day the ♢Q might fall and you have eleven tricks. If not, cash the ♠A, in case the ♠Q is singleton, then ruff your ♢J and take the spade finesse. If that works you again have twelve tricks.

Tip 89: When you have two ways to try for an extra trick, take the line which offers the best chance of success without jeopardising the contract or a good match-point score.

90 Dealer West : Nil vulnerable

WEST	EAST	W	N	E	S
♠ A 10 4 2	♠ 8 7	1NT	2◇ (1)	3♣ (2)	3♡
♡ A K 10	♡ 5	3NT	No	No	No
◇ J 10 9	◇ A K Q 8 7 4	(1) Both majors			
♣ K 10 7	♣ Q 8 4 2	(2) Transfer to diamonds (see Tip 45)			

North leads the ♠K, ducked by West and continues with the ♠Q. South has played ♠6, ♠9, discouraging. You take the ♠A and play the ◇J, ◇10. All follow. How do you continue?

The deal arose in the final of the 2002 World Women's Pairs:

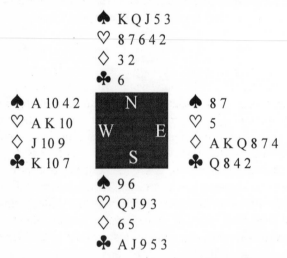

```
              ♠ K Q J 5 3
              ♡ 8 7 6 4 2
              ◇ 3 2
              ♣ 6
♠ A 10 4 2          N          ♠ 8 7
♡ A K 10                       ♡ 5
◇ J 10 9       W       E       ◇ A K Q 8 7 4
♣ K 10 7            S          ♣ Q 8 4 2
              ♠ 9 6
              ♡ Q J 9 3
              ◇ 6 5
              ♣ A J 9 5 3
```

Declarer rattled off the diamonds, cashed ♡A, ♡K to ensure nine tricks and exited with the ♣K. South took the ♣A and cashed one heart, having discarded a heart. +430 was worth a 35% score for E-W.

After diamonds are 2-2, declarer can place North with at most two clubs. Play a club to the queen and ace. When South returns a heart, take ♡A, ♡K and run the diamonds. Later finesse the ♣10 (in fact, South is squeezed in hearts and clubs). +460 would be worth 70%.

Tip 90: A good chance for an overtrick is worth a slight risk.

Part 5: DEFENCE

This is an excellent area on which to concentrate. Players who can defend well have a significant edge. The standard of defence among most players is lower than other areas of their game. Most players can handle constructive bidding competently and can play the dummy reasonably well. When it comes to defending, many adopt a futile line or slop trick after trick. It is no compliment for a defender to be known as a 'magician', one who makes tricks disappear.

At rubber bridge or teams, your task as a defender is clear: defeat the contract. If it happens to cost an overtrick, too bad. You are prepared to sacrifice an overtrick or two for even a remote chance of putting the contract down.

At match-points, defence is far, far tougher. Your object may not be to defeat the contract at all. You may achieve a good score if you can restrict declarer to, say, ten tricks in 3NT instead of allowing eleven tricks. When dummy appears, try to work out whether declarer is likely to succeed. Count dummy's HCP, estimate declarer's points. Does declarer seem to have ample strength for success? If so, your aim is to limit the overtricks. Have they bid a game or a slam with very few points? Then you will need to go all out to defeat the contract. Try to judge the popularity of the contract. If few pairs are likely to bid this game or slam, it will hardly matter whether you concede an overtrick. Defeating their contract will be your objective.

Good defence is often a matter of partnership co-operation. Strong partnerships spend time and effort on their signalling agreements. During play, pay close attention to partner's signals. In defence you can do with all the help you can get.

One of the most important aspects in match-point defence is 'Take your tricks'. When it comes clear that you cannot defeat the contract, make sure that none of the tricks you could take go begging.

91

Dealer East

Nil vulnerable

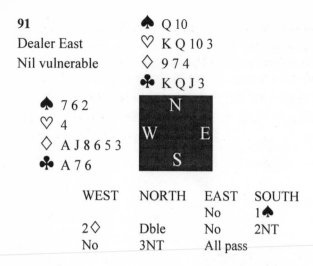

♠ Q 10
♡ K Q 10 3
◇ 9 7 4
♣ K Q J 3

♠ 7 6 2
♡ 4
◇ A J 8 6 5 3
♣ A 7 6

WEST	NORTH	EAST	SOUTH
		No	1♠
2◇	Dble	No	2NT
No	3NT	All pass	

Lead: ◇6 – 4 – 10 – king. South plays the ♣5: 6 – king – 2 and leads dummy's ♠Q: king – ace – 2. Next comes the ♣10 from South. You take the ace and East follows with the ♣4. What next?

East's play of the ◇10 at trick 1 marks South with the ◇Q as well as the ◇K. Should you try to find East's entry to play a diamond through South? That's what happened at the table, but it was a serious blunder. These were the other cards:

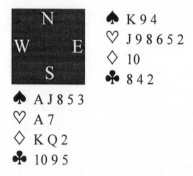

♠ K 9 4
♡ J 9 8 6 5 2
◇ 10
♣ 8 4 2

♠ A J 8 5 3
♡ A 7
◇ K Q 2
♣ 10 9 5

After taking the ♣A, West should cash the ◇A. That holds 3NT to eleven tricks and would have received an average score. When West switched to a heart, South made twelve tricks and only 25% for E-W.

126

After taking the ♣A West should cash the ◇A for two reasons: firstly, if East has a second diamond, South began with ◇K-Q bare and the ◇Q will fall under the ace; secondly, South is sure to have the ♡A to justify the opening bid and 2NT rebid and if West fails to take the ◇A, it may be lost forever, as proved to be the case.

Cover West and South below. East opened 1♡, 1NT from South and 3NT by North. West leads the ♡4. How would you defend as East?

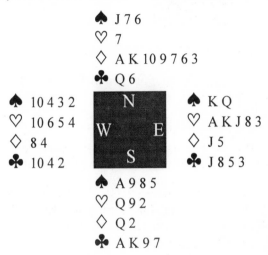

```
              ♠ J 7 6
              ♡ 7
              ◇ A K 10 9 7 6 3
              ♣ Q 6
♠ 10 4 3 2        N        ♠ K Q
♡ 10 6 5 4    W       E    ♡ A K J 8 3
◇ 8 4              S       ◇ J 5
♣ 10 4 2                   ♣ J 8 5 3
              ♠ A 9 8 5
              ♡ Q 9 2
              ◇ Q 2
              ♣ A K 9 7
```

6◇ is on for North-South, but no pair found that in the final of a national pairs championship in 2003. The vast majority were in 3NT. East should take the ♡K and cash the ♡A for a score of 50%.

One East took the ♡K and continued with a low heart. South played the ♡Q and now made twelve tricks. Second bottom to East-West. Even worse was the East who inserted the ♡J at trick 1. South won and cashed the diamonds, catching East in a black-suit squeeze for all the tricks. Bottom score to East-West.

East has 15 HCP and can see 10 HCP in dummy. South has to have the rest for the 1NT overcall and so the diamonds are running. East should foresee the risk in not taking the winners at once.

Tip 91: Take the tricks that are yours unless they cannot vanish.

92 At rubber bridge or teams, you may risk conceding an overtrick when switching to a new suit if that suit offers the best chance of defeating the contract. At pairs, such a risk is usually not warranted. Be very confident of your ground before you switch to any of the suits as East on the layouts below.

(A)	NORTH (Dummy)	(B)	NORTH (Dummy)
	J 6 2		J 6 2
	EAST		EAST
	Q 9 3		K 9 5

If East shifts to this suit, East runs the risk of hitting these layouts:

(A1)   J 6 2   Declarer has two tricks. If East leads the
10 7 5 4   Q 9 3   suit, declarer might play low from hand
    A K 8   and score three tricks.

(A2)   J 6 2   Declarer has one trick and cannot score
K 8 7 5   Q 9 3   two tricks unless one of the defenders
    A 10 4   leads the suit first.

If East leads low, South ducks and West wins. South can later finesse against East for the queen.

(A3)   J 6 2   Declarer has one trick only and cannot
A 8 7 5   Q 9 3   legitimately score two tricks without the
    K 10 4   help of the defence.

If East leads low, South ducks and whether West wins or not, South can make two tricks by finessing the 10 later.

(B1)   J 6 2   Declarer has two tricks. If East leads the
10 8 7 4   K 9 5   suit, declarer can play low from hand and
    A Q 3   score three tricks.

(B2)   J 6 2   Declarer has no trick and cannot come to
A 10 8 4   K 9 5   a trick by leading this suit from either
    Q 7 3   hand. If East or West leads the suit,
                     South scores one trick.

	K 9 6		Declarer has two tricks and will make
Q 7 5		10 8 4 3	only two by finessing the jack. If either
	A J 2		defender leads the suit, declarer can
			make three tricks.

This suit may seem innocuous to East, but if East leads the suit, declarer plays low from hand and scores three tricks. In all the situations so far, East has an honour card and dummy has the card immediately below it. That makes the switch dangerous.

Do not confuse the preceding positions with 'surround' plays. A surround position exists when you sit over a high card, you have that card surrounded (the one above and the one below) and you also have a higher non-touching honour. In these situations, switching to the card above the surrounded card is sound play. For example:

	J 6 4		East is over dummy's jack and has the
8 5 2		A Q 10 7	jack surrounded with the Q-10, and has a
	K 9 3		higher honour as well.

If East wants to lead this suit, the correct card is the queen. South covers and the king wins. Now East has the A-10 over dummy's jack. If West can lead the suit later, East takes the rest of the tricks in this suit and holds declarer to just one trick. If East leads a low card initially or switches to ace and another, South ducks and makes two tricks.

	9 5 2		East is over dummy's 9 and has the 9
Q 6 3		K 10 8 4	surrounded, plus a higher honour as well.
	A J 7		East should shift to the 10.

This holds South to just one trick. If East starts with the 4 or 8, South ducks in hand. West wins, but South can come to a second trick by finessing the jack later.

Tip 92: When you have an honour card and sit over dummy which has the card below your honour, be very wary about switching to this suit. There is a significant risk of giving declarer an extra trick. Note the difference and the correct play when a surround position exists.

93

Dealer North

Both vulnerable

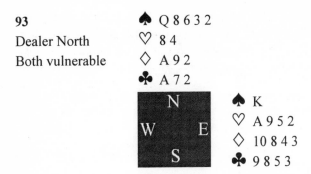

♠ Q 8 6 3 2
♡ 8 4
◇ A 9 2
♣ A 7 2

♠ K
♡ A 9 5 2
◇ 10 8 4 3
♣ 9 8 5 3

South opens 1♠ in third seat, North jumps to 3♠ and South's 4♠ becomes the contract. West leads the ♡Q and East wins with the ace, South following with the ♡3. How should East continue?

Clearly South has the ♡K, but there is no rush to attack either minor as declarer has no obvious discards for either minor. Can a switch be dangerous? Just take a look at the missing cards

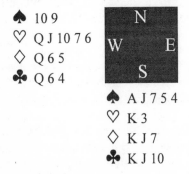

♠ 10 9
♡ Q J 10 7 6
◇ Q 6 5
♣ Q 6 4

♠ A J 7 5 4
♡ K 3
◇ K J 7
♣ K J 10

You cannot beat 4♠, but the results will range from ten to twelve tricks. Your job is to hold South to the minimum number. If you return a heart South can make eleven tricks safely: ♡K; diamond to the ace; trump; draw the last trump; cash the ◇K; exit with the ◇J.

Some declarers will try for twelve tricks by returning to dummy after trumps have been drawn and finessing the ◇J. West wins and exits safely with a diamond. Declarer can make eleven tricks by guessing the clubs, but ten tricks will be the result if declarer mispicks clubs.

However, if East switches to a minor, South is assured of a good result. If you shift to a club, you eliminate the club guess and declarer has eleven tricks. If you try a diamond it is even worse (see Tip 92 and you will see why). Declarer plays low from hand and has no diamond loser. If declarer picks the clubs correctly, declarer will have twelve tricks and East-West will have a bottom board.

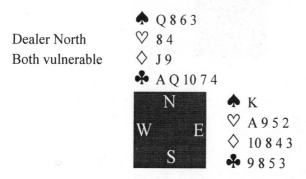

Dealer North

Both vulnerable

♠ Q 8 6 3
♡ 8 4
♢ J 9
♣ A Q 10 7 4

♠ K
♡ A 9 5 2
♢ 10 8 4 3
♣ 9 8 5 3

Same bidding: No : 1♠, 3♠ : 4♠ and same lead, ♡Q from West. East wins with the ace, South following with the ♡3. How should East continue?

The situation is vastly different because this time dummy has a long, strong suit, which declarer may use to discard losers after trumps have been cleared. When dummy has a long, threatening suit, you must take your tricks quickly or possibly not at all. A heart return is futile as South is known to hold the ♡K. The only likely source of tricks is from the diamonds and you should switch to a diamond at trick 2.

South held: ♠ A J 10 5 4   ♡ K 6 3   ♢ K 7 6   ♣ K 6

You cannot defeat 4♠, but you can restrict the overtricks. If you return a heart South can make twelve tricks. On the diamond return, West can take two diamond tricks, South is held to ten tricks and you have taken what's yours.

Tip 93: Beware of switching to a new suit if dummy has no long suit which can provide useful discards for declarer. Take your tricks quickly if dummy does have such a suit.

94
Dealer North
Both vulnerable

♠ A 6
♡ K J 7 3
♢ A Q 5
♣ Q J 6 4

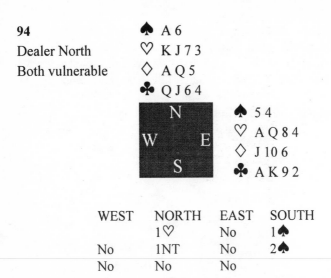

♠ 5 4
♡ A Q 8 4
♢ J 10 6
♣ A K 9 2

WEST	NORTH	EAST	SOUTH
	1♡	No	1♠
No	1NT	No	2♠
No	No	No	

West leads the ♣8: 4 – king – 10. East cashes the ♣A, West following with the ♣3. East continues with the ♣9 (high card for the higher suit back) and West ruffs. West switches to the ♡2: king – ace – 9. How should East continue?

In giving count signals, you can use standard count (lowest from an odd number of cards and high-low with an even number) or reverse signals (lowest from an even number, high-low with an odd number). Reverse signals are slightly superior, since you cannot always afford the top card from a doubleton. Count signals are useful in a cashout position and in such cases it is unlikely to matter whether you play standard count or reverse count.

In the problem above it seems natural to play another club, partly to eliminate this winner, partly because playing the ♡Q is dangerous if South began with a singleton and partly to give partner a chance to over-ruff declarer. However, there may be a better play at trick 5 than another club. Is there anything to guide you?

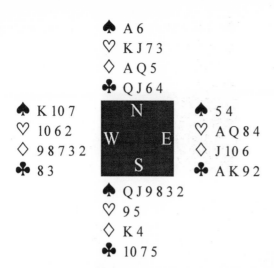

♠ A 6
♥ K J 7 3
♦ A Q 5
♣ Q J 6 4

♠ K 10 7
♥ 10 6 2
♦ 9 8 7 3 2
♣ 8 3

♠ 5 4
♥ A Q 8 4
♦ J 10 6
♣ A K 9 2

♠ Q J 9 8 3 2
♥ 9 5
♦ K 4
♣ 10 7 5

East should cash the ♥Q at trick 5. This gives the defence five tricks and then the fourth club will give West a trump trick. If East plays the fourth club before cashing the second heart, South discards the other heart loser. West will ruff, but declarer will make the rest for +110.

The problem for East is that West's ♥2 could be from 10-6-5-2 or 10-6-2 or 10-5-2. Declarer did well to play as though holding a singleton (rising with the ♥K and dropping the ♥9) and many an East would be misled. If the ♥2 is from 10-6-5-2 it would be a disaster to play the ♥Q. South would ruff and score nine tricks.

Whatever your normal methods for leads from 3-card or longer suits, it will pay you in a cashout situation to lead bottom from a 3-card or a 5-card suit (3rd and 5th). Playing 3rd and 5th may not clarify every problem, but it will sort out the position in cashouts much more often than fourth-highest and bottom from honour-x-x. In the above case West leads the ♥2 and when South follows, East knows that West began with exactly three cards. Therefore South has another heart and it is safe to cash the ♥Q before playing the fourth club.

Tip 94: In a cashout position it is important to use count signals to enable partner to tell the number of cards that can be cashed safely. 3rd and 5th is a good system of leads in a cashout position.

95

Dealer East

Both vulnerable

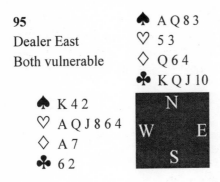

	♠ A Q 8 3
	♡ 5 3
	◇ Q 6 4
	♣ K Q J 10

♠ K 4 2
♡ A Q J 8 6 4
◇ A 7
♣ 6 2

WEST	NORTH	EAST	SOUTH
		1◇	No
1♡	Dble	2NT (1)	No
4NT	No	5♡ (2)	No
6♡	No	No	6♠
Dble	No	No	No

(1) E-W play 2NT over the double as 6 diamonds – 3 hearts
(2) Two key cards for hearts, no ♡Q

West leads the ◇A and another diamond. Dummy plays low and East wins with the ◇9. East switches to the ♡10, which wins the trick, followed by the ♡K, which also wins. East then plays the ◇K, ruffed by South with the ♠J. What would you do as West?

Situations such as these are quite well known:

```
        6 4              If East leads a suit where South and
Q 9 3 2        5         West are void and South ruffs with the 7
    A K J 10 8 7          or 8, West should over-ruff with the 9.
```

If South ruffs with the jack or ten, over-ruffing with the queen gives West one trick only, while discarding gives West two tricks.

```
        J                If given a chance to over-ruff dummy
10 9          Q 7 5 3    East should decline. The queen will win
    A K 8 6 4 2           anyway. There are layouts where East can
                         score a second trick by not over-ruffing.
```

If East does over-ruff here, East scores one trick only.

134

Back to the defensive problem. If South knew the location of the
♠K, West must take the ♠K or not score it at all. On the bidding the
♠K could well be with East and at the table West did well by
discarding a club on the ♠J without any hint of having a problem.

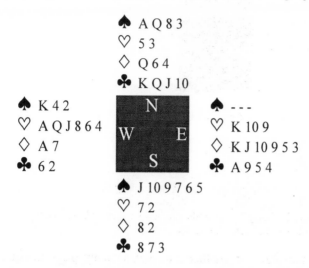

```
                    ♠ A Q 8 3
                    ♡ 5 3
                    ◇ Q 6 4
                    ♣ K Q J 10
    ♠ K 4 2              N              ♠ - - -
    ♡ A Q J 8 6 4                       ♡ K 10 9
    ◇ A 7          W         E          ◇ K J 10 9 5 3
    ♣ 6 2                                ♣ A 9 5 4
                        S
                    ♠ J 10 9 7 6 5
                    ♡ 7 2
                    ◇ 8 2
                    ♣ 8 7 3
```

Declarer took the bait and led a spade to the ace, hoping to drop the
singleton ♠K with East. When West won the next spade, a club went
to East's ace and West was able to ruff the club return.

West knew East had the ♣A for the 1◇ opening. Had West over-
ruffed the ♠J, the defence would take six tricks and score 1400, less
than the 1460 available in 6♡. Clearly not everyone would be
sacrificing on the South hand and so West felt there would be little
match-point difference between +1400 and +1100. Both would
outscore those in game and finish behind those in 6♡. It was worth
the risk of collecting only 1100 for a chance of putting 6♠ doubled
seven down via the club ruff and scoring an absolute top with +1700.

**Tip 95: There are many situations where you can gain an extra
trick by declining to over-ruff declarer. This may occur by
promoting another trump in your hand or because declarer
misplaces the trump honours.**

96
Dealer South
Nil vulnerable

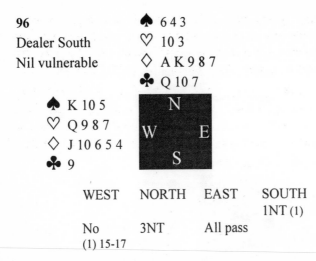

♠ 6 4 3
♡ 10 3
◇ A K 9 8 7
♣ Q 10 7

♠ K 10 5
♡ Q 9 8 7
◇ J 10 6 5 4
♣ 9

WEST	NORTH	EAST	SOUTH
			1NT (1)
No	3NT	All pass	
(1) 15-17			

Judging that dummy would not hold a major and figured to have length in the minors, West led the ♡7 rather than a diamond. Declarer played low from dummy and captured East's ♡K. Next came the ♣A and another club to the ♣10. What would you discard as West?

This was the full deal, which arose in a national championship in 2002:

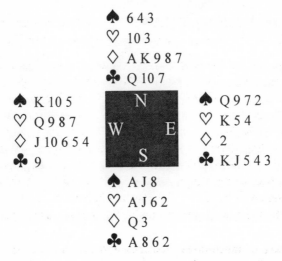

♠ 6 4 3
♡ 10 3
◇ A K 9 8 7
♣ Q 10 7

♠ K 10 5
♡ Q 9 8 7
◇ J 10 6 5 4
♣ 9

♠ Q 9 7 2
♡ K 5 4
◇ 2
♣ K J 5 4 3

♠ A J 8
♡ A J 6 2
◇ Q 3
♣ A 8 6 2

With no easy discard, West chose the ◇4, just as many would do.

When defending against no-trumps and required to make an early discard, most defenders discard from a 5+ suit. An expert will note the discard, take the inference and possibly base a whole line of play on that card. That's what Australian champion Bob Richman did on this deal.

East won with the ♣J and returned the ♡5. West took the ♡Q (ducking is better) and returned a heart, taken by the ♡J. Richman now led a club to the queen and West discarded the ♠5. East took the ♣K and shifted to the ♠2. Richman rose with the ♠A, leaving this position:

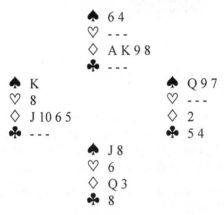

So far declarer had taken four tricks. He had a club winner and three diamond tricks but still needed one more. Where could he find that?

When Richman cashed the ♣8, what was West to throw? Unable to afford either red suit, West threw the ♠K. Richman now pondered over the ◇4 discard. Could the ◇4 be a deceptive card from J-6-5-4-2 or 10-6-5-4-2? Reading the ◇4 as lowest from five diamonds and hence from ◇J-10-6-5-4, Richman led the ◇3, ◇5 from West, and inserted the ◇8 from dummy. When that held, he played the ◇9 to his ◇Q and exited with the ♡6. That gave the lead to West who, with only diamonds left, became the stepping-stone for declarer to reach dummy. (Had West inserted ◇10 or ◇J, the play would have been easier and the outcome the same, with West becoming the stepping-stone again.)

Tip 96: Beware of mechanical discards and try to avoid making your first discard from a 5-card suit against an expert declarer.

97
Dealer South
Both vulnerable

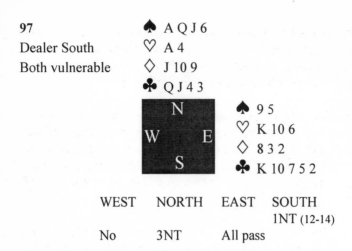

♠ A Q J 6
♡ A 4
◇ J 10 9
♣ Q J 4 3

♠ 9 5
♡ K 10 6
◇ 8 3 2
♣ K 10 7 5 2

WEST	NORTH	EAST	SOUTH
			1NT (12-14)
No	3NT	All pass	

West leads the ♡Q and declarer plays the ace from dummy. Which card should East play?

We all know Murphy's First Law of Defence: 'If you give partner a chance to go wrong, partner will take that chance.' There are many occasions when partner will lead from an honour sequence and will be unable to tell whether you or declarer has the missing honour. If you can clarify the position without loss, do so. The full deal looks like this:

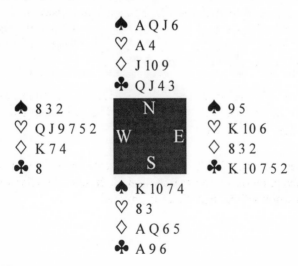

♠ A Q J 6
♡ A 4
◇ J 10 9
♣ Q J 4 3

♠ 8 3 2
♡ Q J 9 7 5 2
◇ K 7 4
♣ 8

♠ 9 5
♡ K 10 6
◇ 8 3 2
♣ K 10 7 5 2

♠ K 10 7 4
♡ 8 3
◇ A Q 6 5
♣ A 9 6

138

In addition, partner will expect your co-operation and if it is not forthcoming, partner will place the missing honour with declarer. You will have to answer to the charge of being declarer's accomplice if you fail to drop your honour card when appropriate.

At the table East followed with the ♡6 (East-West were using reverse signals where lowest is encouraging), but that was no success. Declarer continued with the ◇J and West won with the ◇K. West switched to a spade and not only was the contract not heavily defeated, but East-West also scored a near bottom, as South's 3NT outscored most of those in the normal 4♠.

East should play the ♡10 to clear up the heart position for West. East knows that West has led from a Q-J-9 sequence, but West does not know East's holding. The 10 will solidify West's suit so that West will know it is safe to play a second heart no matter where the king is.

Dropping the ♡6 as a come-on signal may be clear to East, but West might well read it as a singleton. That would give South ♡K-10-8-3, certainly a possibility, and now a second round of hearts would give declarer a gift of a third heart trick.

Dropping the ♡K is better than the ♡6, but that is also risky. Again, partner might read this as a singleton, giving South ♡10-8-6-3. If West cashes the ♡J when in with the ◇K, it would give South an extra heart trick, which South could not have developed.

The ♡10 allows West to continue the hearts without risk. Then East can overtake with the ♡K and return the ♡6. That will teach North to seek the major-suit fit next time.

Tip 97: When partner leads from an interior sequence or a broken sequence, be quick to drop an honour if you can afford it so that the position will be clarified for partner.

98
Dealer East
Nil vulnerable

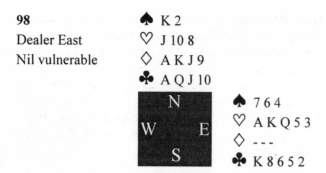

♠ K 2
♡ J 10 8
♢ A K J 9
♣ A Q J 10

♠ 7 6 4
♡ A K Q 5 3
♢ - - -
♣ K 8 6 5 2

With neither side vulnerable, East opens 1♡, South jumps to 2♠ (weak jump-overcall), West passes and North's 4♠ is passed out. West leads the ♡9. How should East plan the defence? Be specific about the cards East is to play.

West's ♡9 is clearly from a singleton or a doubleton. East wants a diamond ruff and can put West back on lead by taking two hearts and forcing West to ruff the third heart. (West might not ruff if you play the top three hearts.) To indicate that East wants a diamond ruff, not a club ruff, East plays ♡A, ♡K (abnormal order) and then ♡5. By playing highest card each time, East is asking for the higher suit outside trumps.

Dealer East
Nil vulnerable

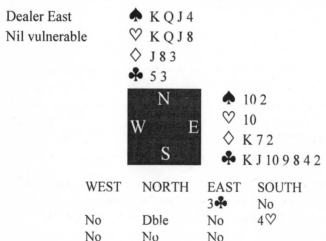

♠ K Q J 4
♡ K Q J 8
♢ J 8 3
♣ 5 3

♠ 10 2
♡ 10
♢ K 7 2
♣ K J 10 9 8 4 2

WEST	NORTH	EAST	SOUTH
		3♣	No
No	Dble	No	4♡
No	No	No	

West leads the ♣7. How would you plan the defence as East?

The ♣7 lead is a singleton or top from a doubleton and so South has ♣A-Q-6 or ♣A-Q. Your card is therefore irrelevant in terms of trick-taking ability. South will make two club tricks no matter which card you play. If the lead is a singleton, West needs to know your entry and the ◇K is the only possibility. East should therefore play the ♣2, lowest card for the lower suit entry. This simple signal would not occur to some players, who would mechanically play third-hand-high. They thus miss a golden opportunity to furnish partner with highly useful information.

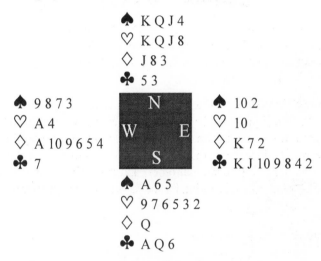

```
            ♠ K Q J 4
            ♡ K Q J 8
            ◇ J 8 3
            ♣ 5 3
♠ 9 8 7 3        N        ♠ 10 2
♡ A 4                     ♡ 10
◇ A 10 9 6 5 4   W    E   ◇ K 7 2
♣ 7              S        ♣ K J 10 9 8 4 2
            ♠ A 6 5
            ♡ 9 7 6 5 3 2
            ◇ Q
            ♣ A Q 6
```

At the table East did play the ♣2 and West understood the message. West won the heart lead at trick 2 and switched to the ◇9. East's king won and, deducing that the ◇9 denied interest in a diamond return, East returned a club, ruffed. South ruffed the ◇A next and made 4♡ for +420, but this neat defence was worth a near-top for East-West. There were many 450s to North-South on the score-sheet.

Had West started with ♣7-6, when there is no club ruff, West would shift to ◇A and another diamond. If East had a void in spades, East might play the ♣J on trick 1, high card asking for the higher suit.

Tip 98: When your play within a suit is immaterial, the card you play can be helpful as a suit-preference signal.

99
Dealer East
Both vulnerable

♠	A 9 6 3	
♡	Q 4	
◇	10 9 5 4	
♣	K 7 2	

```
        N
   W        E          ♠ 2
        S              ♡ 5 3
                       ◇ K Q J 7
                       ♣ J 9 8 6 4 3
```

WEST	NORTH	EAST	SOUTH
		No	1♣ (1)
No	1NT	No	2♣ (2)
No	2♡ (3)	No	3♠ (4)
No	4♠ (5)	No	4NT
No	5◇	No	6♠
No	No	No	

(1) Precision system, artificial, strong club
(2) Inquiry about responder's major suit holdings
(3) Shows four spades
(4) Sets spades as trumps
(5) No cue-bid means no ace outside trumps

The auction is complex, but that is par for the course at duplicate. Make sure you understand the auction before your opening lead. You are entitled to ask for and receive a full explanation of their bidding.

Lead: ◇2 (3rd and 5th). East's ◇J is taken by the ace. South cashes the ♠K: 4 – 3 – 2, and the ♠Q: 5 – 6 – club discard by East. South continues with the ◇8: 3 – 5 – queen. What should East play next?

A primary signal is the signal given by the first card you play in a given suit, whether it is an attitude signal or a count signal. If you then have more than one card left in that suit, the next card played (the second card or the secondary signal) can be used to send a suit-preference message. Suppose you have played the 2 from 9-4-2. On the next round you can play the 9 (preference for the higher suit) or the 4 (no strong preference for the higher suit).

Back to East's problem in 6♠. It may be vital for East to find the right switch at this moment. What are the clues? West's ◇2 lead, 3rd and 5th, is now known to be from a 3-card suit, 6-3-2. On the next lead of diamonds, West followed with the ◇3. The lowest remaining diamond implies interest in the lower suit outside trumps (or at least no strong interest in the higher outside suit). East should therefore shift to a club. With a strong desire for a heart switch, West would have played the ◇6 on the second round of diamonds.

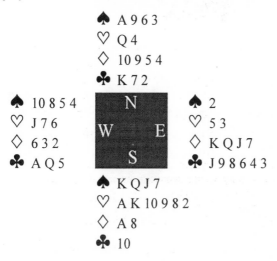

```
                    ♠ A 9 6 3
                    ♡ Q 4
                    ◇ 10 9 5 4
                    ♣ K 7 2
   ♠ 10 8 5 4          N          ♠ 2
   ♡ J 7 6                        ♡ 5 3
   ◇ 6 3 2        W       E       ◇ K Q J 7
   ♣ A Q 5            S           ♣ J 9 8 6 4 3
                    ♠ K Q J 7
                    ♡ A K 10 9 8 2
                    ◇ A 8
                    ♣ 10
```

Defending is very difficult when very little is known about declarer's hand and you must make good use of signalling opportunities. West hit on the diamond lead, the only suit to shoot the slam. When the bad break in spades turned up, declarer led the ◇8, hoping that the ♣A would not be with the player who won this trick. Declarer's plan was to win, say, a heart return with the queen, ruff a diamond high, finesse the ♠9, draw the last trump and then run the hearts.

West's ♠4, then ♠5, lowest trump each time, was also intended as a secondary signal, asking for clubs. When you can afford it, such secondary suit-preference messages are available in the trump suit.

Tip 99: You may be able to help partner find the best switch by the use of secondary suit-preference signals.

100 You are in the middle game and East shifts to this suit. What action should West take?

(a)   NORTH (Dummy)   East switches to the jack and
              Q 7 2   South plays low.

WEST
A 9 3   What should West do?

(b)   NORTH (Dummy)   East switches to the ten and
              A J 2   South plays low.

WEST
K 8 3   What should West do?

(a) If East has led from K-J-10-x, West must rise with the ace, but if East has led from J-10-x-x, West should play low. To play the ace this time would give South two tricks. How can West tell?

(b) If East's 10 is from Q-10-9-x, West should rise with the king, but if East has 10-9-x-x, West should play low. How can West tell?

These positions are ambiguous and without agreements here, West has to guess what to do. As you do not want to give declarer an undeserved trick, it is worth distinguishing East's holdings. You can achieve this by agreeing to lead top or third from the relevant holdings.

(a) From K-J-10-x, East switches to the 10. If South has the king and jack it cannot hurt West to take the ace and if East has K-J-10-x, it is vital to do so. The 10 lead means West has no problem. From J-10-x-x East leads the jack. West knows from the jack that East cannot have K-J-10-x and so West will play low.

(b) From Q-10-9-x, East leads the 9 (third). When South plays low, West knows to play the king. If East has Q-10-9-x playing the king is essential and if South has the Q and 10, playing the king does not cost. From 10-9-x-x East leads the 10 (top). West can tell that East does not have Q-10-9-x and so plays low, restricting South to two tricks.

Tip 100: When sitting over dummy and switching to an honour when dummy has a key honour, leading third from an interior sequence or top of other sequences clarifies the position for partner.